The Politics of International Trade

The Politics of International Trade

초판 1쇄 발행 2020년 2월 28일
초판 2쇄 발행 2024년 2월 20일

지 은 이 James C. Schopf
펴 낸 이 신일희
펴 낸 곳 계명대학교 출판부
출판등록 제347-1998-1호(1970. 9. 1)
주　　소 대구광역시 달서구 달구벌대로 1095
대표전화 053-580-6233
팩　　스 053-580-6235
홈페이지 www.kmupress.com

ISBN 979-11-6516-038-8 93340 정가 23,000원

이 도서의 국립중앙도서관 출판예정도서목록(CIP)은 서지정보유통지원시스템 홈페이지(http://seoji.nl.go.kr)와 국가자료종합목록 구축시스템(http://kolis-net.nl.go.kr)에서 이용하실 수 있습니다. (CIP제어번호 : CIP2020007972)

The Politics of International Trade

James C. Schopf

Preface

This is the first textbook specifically designed to teach 한국외교론 in English to Korean students, fulfilling two objectives: helping students to learn the theories, principles, historic events, and actors central to the discipline, while simultaneously aiming to improve English comprehension and expand vocabulary.

The book begins by introducing the principles, assumptions, causal logic and supporting evidence related to the three main theories within the field: Liberalism, Realism, and Marxism/Structuralism. The text next analyzes the field with theoretical explanations categorized according to the level of analysis, starting with societal groups, and then moving to domestic institutions, the international systemic distribution of power and finally to international institutions. Before concluding, the book uses historical cases to test the explanatory power of these different approaches.

The text is supplemented by 265 review questions, provided at the bottom of the page, which highlight key points. Review questions are used as prompts for English writing exercises and guide students preparing for the mid-term and final exams. 237 vocabulary matching exercises spread throughout the book prepare students for difficult vocabulary in the upcoming text and ease reading. Students requiring further assistance can consult the extensive glossary in the back of the book for correct definitions.

CONTENTS

1 Introduction: The Focus of the Book

2 Introduction to Theory

3 Liberal Theory

4 Realism

5 Marxism / Structural Theory

Part I

Introduction and Theory

Chapter

1 Introduction: The Focus of the Book

This book focuses on the theory and practice of international trade policy and politics. The book seeks to impart knowledge about the major issues, terms and processes involved with trade policy and introduces the major academic schools of trade policy politics. The book begins by introducing the three traditional approaches to trade policy theory: Realism, Liberalism and Marxism, before introducing an alternative, level of analysis categorization scheme of trade politics, beginning with the domestic societal approach, and then examining the domestic institutional (statist) and international approaches to trade policy.

comprises	상호간의
portion	구성하다
mutual	부분
interaction	상호 작용

govern	나눠주다
distribute	작동
operation	형성하다
mold	통치하다

International trade policy comprises a major portion of the study of International Political Economy, which is the study of the mutual interaction between politics and economics. Politics here refers to the state, or the set of institutions and rules, which govern social and economic interactions, while the economy is the system of producing, distributing, and using wealth. Political economy involves studying the ways in which government policies affect market operations and the economic forces, which mold government policies.

is concerned with	기능	hinder	보호
outcomes	와 관련있다	pressures	방해하다
functioning	결과	classes	계급
substitute	대체	protection	압박

On one hand, I.P.E. is concerned with the effects of government policies on market outcomes. For example, can the government lead economic development, improve the functioning of the market or substitute for the market? Or, does government intervention lead to wasted resources, encourage corruption, or hinder economic development?

I.P.E. also deals with the effects of economic pressures and economic forces on government policy-making. For example, which types of economic groups desire trade protection? Is it business sectors that seek trade protection, or is it economic classes, like workers or farmers?

tension	긴장
sybiosis	추구
sovereignty	공생
pursue	주권

phenomena	불황
recession	환경
currency	통화
environmental	현상

Tension and symbiosis describe relations between the state and the market. On the one hand, the state seeks to preserve national sovereignty and unity while the market pursues economic openness and breaking down of state barriers.

But states also establish rules to protect private property rights and provide the transportation and communication infrastructure necessary for market transactions. The interaction between states and markets produces many important phenomena, including global recessions, currency crises, poverty in developing nations, and global environmental problems.

interdisciplinary	사회학자
sociologists	지리학자
anthropologist	인류학자
geographer	학제간

emerged	세심한 주의를 하다
prominent	부상되다
disintegration	해체
pay close attention	두드러진

I.P.E. is interdisciplinary in nature, and draws on contributions from political scientists, economists, sociologists,

---

- ***What is IPE?***
- ***How does politics affect economics?***
- ***How does economics affect politics?***

anthropologist, historians and geographers.

International Political Economy has emerged as one of the most prominent fields of intellectual activity in the social sciences rose to prominence during the 1970s following the disintegration of stability and prosperity of the first twenty-five years of the postwar period. As economic issues became politicized, politicians also began to pay closer attention to economic trends.

1.1 The Traditional Approaches to Trade Policy: Liberal, Realist and Marxist

In I.P.E., there is no general theory that can simultaneously take into account all relevant factors. Instead there are a variety of partial theories which can explain a narrower range of outcomes. Debates in I.P.E. usually concern which types of partial theories are most helpful for which types of problems.

Liberalism	마르크스주의
Marxism	자유주의
Realism	현실주의
inevitability	불가피한

autonomous	할당
determine	결정
voluntary	자율적
allocation	자발적인

The first section of the book explores the traditional theories of International Political Economy: Liberalism, Marxism and Realism. The three different schools begin with different assumptions about the nature of main actor. Where Liberals focus on individuals and Marxists on class, Realists concentrate on the nation state. The three perspectives also differ on the inevitability of conflict with the political economy, with Liberals emphasizing cooperation and Realists and Marxists predicting conflict. While Liberals believe economics and politics are largely autonomous spheres, Marxists maintain that economics determines politics and Realists argue that politics determines economics.

Liberals advocate free trade and free markets and emphasize, whether through the market or in politics, that all parties can benefit through voluntary exchange. Liberals believe in the superiority of market allocation of scarce resources.

supplying	유지	collusion	자유롭게
maintain	막다	best off	결탁
provide	제공	goods	최선
block	공급	freely	제품

The government's economic role should thus be limited to supplying the conditions necessary to maintain a free market, such as by providing defense and infrastructure, protecting property rights and blocking unfair collusion. Liberals argue that all countries are best off when goods and services move freely across borders.

assertion	본래의	bargaining	착취
maximizes	주장	exploitation	을 받다
inherently	약화시키다	subject to	홍정
undermine	최대화	anarchy	무정부상태

Marxists reject the assertion that exchange between individuals maximizes social welfare and instead see capitalism is an inherently conflictual system in which capitalists exploit labor. Marxists argue that the creation of MNCs have undermined labor's bargaining power and aided international capitalism's exploitation of poor countries.

Realists hold that international relations occur under anarchy, a condition where sovereign nations are subject to no higher authority. Anarchy makes the use of force always possible and prevents nations from relying on others.

concentration	가능성	perspective	관점
likelihood	집중	constraints	내재적
scheme	분리시키다	impose	제약
divide	계획	inherent	부여하다

States must instead defend themselves. Realists argue that states will sacrifice economic gain through trade protection to strengthen their military power, and argue that concentration of power in the international system increases the likelihood of economic openness.

1.2 Levels of Analysis & Trade Policy: Society, State and the International System

Most of the book is devoted to explaining an alternative, level of analysis categorization scheme of trade politics, dividing theories of international trade policy into a domestic societal approach, domestic institutional or statist approach, and international approach.

Scholars who take an international perspective emphasize the constraints imposed on states by the global geo-strategic and diplomatic environment. They focus on the inherent conflict among states in a world in which cooperation is difficult to achieve.

advocates	강조	insulated	우선순위
stress	국가통제주의자	emanate	보호
comprise	지지자	priorities	에서 나오다
statist	구성	deal with	대처하다

Scholars who take a domestic approach differ by looking inside the nation state for explanations of international trade policy. While some advocates of the domestic approach stress importance of the state, the politicians and political institutions that comprise the national government, other scholars focus on private actors in society.

Scholars taking a statist, or domestic institutionalist perspective, view the state as relatively insulated from the many political and economic pressures emanating from society. National leaders, policymakers and the political institutions within which they operate are seen as the main actors determining national priorities and implementing policies, including those dealing with foreign trade.

proponent	도구	determinant	에 근거하여
transmitter	근본	demand	결정 요인
underlying	전달자	radically	급진적으로
tool	지지자	on the basis of	수요

The opposing, domestic societal perspective focuses on economic and sociopolitical actors rather than political leaders. Proponents of the societal view minimize international constraints and view policymakers as little more than the transmitters of underlying societal demands. The state is seen as merely a tool of socioeconomic and political interests. Accordingly the determinants of national policy, including trade policy, are the demands made by individuals, firms, and groups rather than the independent actions of policymakers.

Applying the three views to trends in international trade policy shows how serious scholars can arrive at radically different conclusions on the basis of the same information.

gradually	변화	roots	견딜 수 없는
shift	점차적으로	articulate	정신적충격
cement	강화시키다	trauma	뿌리
bolster	강화하다	intolerable	표현

The international, statist and societal approaches explain long-term changes in trade policy very differently. Between World Wars I and 2 and particularly in the 1930s, almost all European nations and the US were highly protectionist. After WW 2, though, the North American and Western European markets were gradually opened to one another and to the rest of the world.

Scholars supporting international explanations argue that domestic political changes in Europe and the US were too small to explain such a radical shift. The postwar international political role of the US and Western Europe was very different from the 1930s, since the North American and Western European countries were united in alliance against the Soviet Union. Free trade between Atlantic allies helped to cement the alliance and bolster it against the Soviet Union.

Scholars who promote domestic level explanations argue that since the US and its allies created a free trade system through the Marshall Plan, Bretton Wood agreement and the European Union, scholars must search within states for the roots of trade policy. Statist scholars argue that trade liberalization arose out of national security concerns as understood and articulated by a small number of political leaders and officials in the US and Western European governments who went about selling free trade policies to their publics. The trauma of the Great Depression had taught these leaders that protectionism would produce intolerable social tensions.

exert	출현	counter productive	무게
socioeconomic	다국적	relative	상대적
multinational	가하다	weight	정당화
emerge	사회경제적	justification	생산에 역행하다

The explanation goes to the opinions, beliefs, and desires of national political leaders for free trade.

Domestic society oriented scholars, on the other hand, focus on the policy pressures exerted by various socioeconomic groups, some desiring free trade and others backing protection from imports. For important new groups, like multinational corporations, which emerged during the interwar period, trade protection was counter productive because it limited access to the world economy. In contrast, free trade opened up new profitable possibilities for American and Western European firms.

While all scholars recognize that the foreign economic policies of all countries are constrained by both international and domestic factors, disagreement concerns the relative weights to be assigned to each set of causes.

So, the book starts by reviewing the main theories in I.P.E., analyzing the Liberal, Realist and Marxist views of trade, then examines the different tools of trade policy, and different justifications for trade protection.

After addressing the traditional theoretical explanations for trade policy, the book explores theories of trade policy based on level of analysis, beginning with the domestic societal view, and then moving to domestic institutional and international systemic approaches, concluding with an exploration of the rise of regional trade agreements, or RTAs.

Chapter

2 Introduction to Theory

This chapter introduces two different types of theories: normative and positive, defining the concept of theory, and discussing the appropriate method by which to evaluate a theory. There are two types of theories in I.P.E.: normative theory and positive theory

2.1 The Normative or 'Policy' Approach

Normative theory, which is also called the 'Policy Approach,' is not the approach we will usually use in this book, since much of the work in this approach to I.P.E. seeks to influence government policy decisions. Normative theory, in fact, is not interested in trying to understand the way the international political economy actually works.

prescription	쓸모가 없다
perspective	처방전
what ought to be	무엇이 있어야되는지
worthless	관점

alternative policy	참조
analysis	분석
refer to	결과
outcomes	대안책

Normative theories primarily provide policy prescriptions from different theoretical perspectives, including Realist, Liberal, Marxist approaches, but do not explicitly reveal the theoretic assumptions at their core. The policy advice from this approach takes the form of a normative statement about what ought to be, but does not explain what actually happened. As an example of the normative approach, take the statement that "Korea should lower tariffs to grow the economy." A normative statement of this kind is worthless without analytical support. In fact, in order to recommend a policy, its proponent should first make a prediction about a policy's effects. Then the scholar should compare the policy's effects with the outcomes produced from alternative policies. So, in our example about Korea and tariffs, we must first know the effect of trade on economic growth. Learning about the effects of trade require analysis across time and different cases. Without analysis, a normative statement is merely someone's personal opinion.

2.2 The Positive or Analytical Perspective

The positive or analytical perspective is taken by most of the scholars we refer to in this book. The positive approach seeks to explain variation in important economic or political outcomes.

evaluate	현상	independent variable	종속 변수
hypothesis	변수	causal	원인이 되는
variable	평가하다	dependent variable	결과
phenomena	가설	resulting	독립 변수

So, how can we define and evaluate theories? What is a positive theory? A positive theory is a hypothesis for how variable A causes variable B. There must be at least two variables in any positive theory. Variables are phenomena that change. The first variable is called the 'Independent Variable.' It is the causal variable. It is denoted by the letter A. The other variable is the 'Dependent Variable.' It is the resulting variable, known as B.

assumption	가정	maximize	현실적인
simplify	행위자	testable	시험할 수 있는
actors	동기	realistic	추상적인
motivation	단순화하다	abstract	극대화하다

- ***What is the difference between normative and positive theory?***

All positive theories also make assumptions in order to simplify reality. Assumptions define the actors and determine the actor's motivations. For instance, classic liberal economie theories assume that actors are individuals. This type of theory assumes that people are motivated to maximize wealth. Of course this is not true for everyone, but a theory has to be simple in order to be testable.

Some think that a theory's assumptions should be realistic. All assumptions will be always be incomplete to some degree, by definition, however, because any abstract simplification of reality is not realistic.

logical	생성합니다	decent	비평
empirical	실제적	Structuralism	구조주의
accuracy	논리적	critique	중상주의
yields	정확성	Mercantilism	괜찮은

A theory must also be logical. There should be a logical process from the cause to the result. We judge a theory, therefore, according to the empirical accuracy of its predictions when tested against evidence, not by how realistic its assumptions are. If a theory yields accurate predictions, we can conclude that it is a decent theory. In the next section we will examine three groups of I.P.E. theories, including Liberalism,

---

- ***What is an independent variable?***
- ***What is a dependent variable?***

Realism, and Marxism, which is also known as Structuralism.

- ***How can we evaluate a positive theory?***

Chapter

3 Liberal Theory

Liberalism is the most influential perspective in I.P.E., and this theoretic tradition has a long history, originally arising as a critique of mercantilism under Adam Smith and David Ricardo.

organizations	제 2 차 세계 대전
World War II	국제 통화 기금
I.M.F.	조직
G.A.T.T.	관세 및 무역에 관한 일반 협정

based	기반으로
domestic	보수주의
contrasted	대조
Conservatism	국내

Liberalism is also the most important theory within international economic organizations, and the major post World War II international economic organizations (I.M.F., World Bank and GATT) are all based on liberal economic principles. The economic policies of most states today are also strongly influenced by liberal principles.

What does the term 'Liberal' mean? The I.P.E. meaning

of the term Liberal is different from the term liberal in U.S. domestic politics.

In U.S. domestic politics, liberalism is often contrasted with conservatism.

progressive	자유 시장	intervention	강조하다
committed to	최소한의	inequality	불평등
free markets	진보적인	emphasize	개입
minimal	옹호한다는	property rights	재산권

On the other hand, liberalism in U.S. domestic politics means to be progressive. While U.S. conservatives are committed to free markets and minimal governmental intervention, U.S. Liberals support greater government involvement in the market to prevent inequality. Liberal economists, though, are similar to U.S. conservatives. Liberal economists emphasize the importance of the free market and private property rights and stress a limited role for government.

tenets	핵심	unitary	계급
core	합리적인	actor	단일
belief	믿음	class	관계
rational	신념	relations	행위자

3.1 The basic tenets of the liberal perspective

The core beliefs of Realism and Marxism are easier to

define than to find the core beliefs of liberalism. Realists focus on the Rational Unitary Actor, while Marxists view the world in terms of class relations. Liberalism, on the other hand, is more complex. Liberalism includes more actors and more levels of analysis than the other two schools of thought.

variants	개입 주의자	negative freedom	제한적인
relevant to	에 관련된	interference	간섭
orthodox	변종	restrictive	부정적인 자유
interventionist	전통적인	focus	초점

Three variants of liberalism are directly relevant to the study of I.P.E., the orthodox, interventionist, and institutional schools of liberalism.

Orthodox liberals want to promote so-called 'negative freedom,' meaning freedom of the private sector and the market, with minimal interference from the state. The earliest economic Liberals like Adam Smith and David Ricardo followed Liberal orthodoxy.

A second school of Liberal thought is known as Interventionist liberalism. These scholars believe that only focusing on negative freedom is too restrictive.

- ***What is the difference between an American liberal and an economic liberal?***

widespread	공정성
benefits	이득
fairness	정의
justice	광범위한

institutionalist	기능
supplement	보완
functioning	사회적인
societal	기관 주의자

This school holds that the private sector and the market do not always produce widespread benefits. Some government involvement, therefore, is necessary to promote more equality, fairness, and justice in a free market economy.

The third group, known as Institutionalist Liberals, argue that international institutions, like the W.T.O, I.M.F. and the World Bank, can supplement the functioning of the market.

3.2 The Assumptions of Liberalism

Liberals premise their argument with assumptions about the role of the individual, the state, and societal groups.

self-interested	서로
unit of analysis	분석 단위
one another	이기적인
consumer	소비자

firm	추구하다
entrepreneur	부
wealth	사업가
pursue	회사

- ***Compare orthodox, interventionist and institutional liberalism.***
- ***For liberals what are the main actors and their motivations?***
- ***How is policy produced, according to liberals?***

Liberalism takes self-interested individuals as its unit of analysis. They interact with one another within nation-states, in the economy, and in politics. Liberalism focuses on society, particularly individual consumers, firms and entrepreneurs. Liberals argue that individuals seek economic wealth, and behave rationally. Policy outcomes are a product of the combined demands of different groups of individuals within society. Liberals also argue that if individuals pursue their own interests, it benefits society.

As Adam Smith pointed out, the market turns individual selfish interest into a societal advantage.

turn	상호
interactions	변환
mutual	상호 작용
positive sum	양의 합계

concerned with	최빈개도국
cooperation	촉진시키다
LDCs	관련된
spur	협력

3.3 The Liberal View of International Trade

As in the domestic level, at the international level, liberals argue that international economic interactions can be mutual beneficial, representing a positive sum game. All states and individuals gain from open economic relationships through markets and market prices, even if they do not gain equally. Liberals are not concerned with which party gains more through cooperation.

3.4 The Liberal View of Development

Liberals believe that all countries will gain from trade, including the Least Developed Countries (LDCs). Liberals view LDCs today, much like European and American nations were in the 1800s and believe that today's LDCs can become advanced nations by following the example of Europe and the U.S. In fact, liberals believe that it is easier for LDCs today to develop than it was for America and Europe.

LDCs in the 21st century have the advantages of advanced technology and modern forms of organization, such as firms. Liberals believe that greater integration with advanced economies will spur modernization and rapid economic growth in LDCs.

isolation	절대적	slice	집행
backwardness	상대적인	limited role	보장
absolute	후진성	enforce	제한된 역할
relative	고립	ensure	조각

Isolation, on the other hand, will lead to backwardness. So, Liberals are concerned with the absolute level of economic growth. They want a bigger overall pie and don't care about the relative size of each country's slice of pie.

- ***Is it bad to be selfish, according to liberals?***

Liberals also think that the state should play a limited role. In the Liberal view, the state's role is simply to enforce property rights to ensure a free market with free competition

public good	방어	figure	재고량
infrastructure	사회 기반 시설	laissez faire	인물
defense	공공재	capability	자유방임주의
liberty	자유	stock	능력

while providing the public goods of infrastructure and defense.

John Locke and Adam Smith were two of the most important Liberal theorists. The Liberal tradition dates back to writings of John Locke (1632 – 1704), who argued that the primary role of the state was to ensure people's liberties and property. Adam Smith (1723-1790) is considered to be the central figure who applied orthodox liberalism to political economy. Smith believed in laissez faire economics and opposed mercantilism, arguing that the real wealth of a nation was its productive capability, not its stock of gold.

zero sum	분담	works best	과세
positive sum	절대 우위	comparative advantage	효율적으로
absolute advantage	제로섬	taxation	비교 우위
division of labor	양의 합계	efficiently	가장 잘 되다

- ***How do liberals view LDCs today?***
- ***What policy do liberals advocate for economic development?***

Smith argued that trade was not a zero sum game. While Mercantilists believed in a zero sum game, meaning that one side's gain of gold represented the other sides, Smith argued that trade was a positive sum, in which all states simultaneously gained. Free trade was best for everyone due to the principle of Absolute Advantage. Trade created a division of labor among people within countries, and among countries in the world market.

Each state could specialize production on what it did best. All parties would benefit from specializing to efficiently produce goods and then gain through trade with others. Smith believed that what works best for a family also works best for a nation. Buying from the cheapest supplier is better than trying to make everything yourself.

David Ricardo (1772-1823) complimented Smith by introducing the idea of Comparative Advantage, strengthening the free trade argument. His 1817 article, "Principles of Political Economy and Taxation," is still cited in international economics textbooks. According to Ricardo a nation will gain from trade even if that nation cannot produce goods more efficiently than other nations.

- ***What do liberals prefer: absolute or relative gain? Why?***
- ***How do Liberals view free trade?***
- ***What is Absolute Advantage?***

foregone	필	better off	물품을
opportunity cost	전문화	item	이동
specialization	기회 비용	exchange	더 나은
bolt	포기했던	shift	교환

Ricardo showed that a nation does not need to have an "Absolute Advantage" to gain from trade. Instead, a nation should specialize in activities where it has a "Comparative Advantage." It should make products in which it has a relative advantage. Comparative Advantage occurs when a country is able to produce an item at a lower cost, in terms of opportunities foregone (opportunity cost) than another country. This is reflected in the price differences of production between countries.

3.5 Absolute Advantage vs. Comparative Advantage

The example of Portugal and England producing wine and cloth illustrates the difference between Absolute and Comparative Advantage and the gains from trade and

---

- ***How is Comparative Advantage different from Absolute Advantage?***
- ***Here is the amount of labor to produce Wine and Cloth in Portugal and England.***

specialization.

(# of Worker days)	1 bottle of Wine	1 bolt of Cloth
England	3 days	7 days
Portugal	1 day	5 days

	Price of 1 bottle of Wine	Price of 1 bolt of Clot
England	(.428) 3/7 bolt of cloth	2.3 (7/3) bottles of wine
Portugal	(.20) 1/5 bolt of cloth	5 bottles of wine

The example illustrates that England possesses no absolute advantage. England is unable to produce wine or cloth as efficiently as Portugal. Yet the two countries have differences in opportunity costs which are reflected in price differences between the two countries.

As a result, England has a comparative advantage in cloth production. Cloth is cheaper in England, even though England has no absolute advantage and cannot produce cloth as efficiently as Portugal. Portugal, on the other hand, has a comparative advantage in wine production. Wine is cheaper in Portugal.

The two sides can also can through exchange with one

- ***Which nation has an absolute advantage in wine production?***
- ***Which nation has an absolute advantage in cloth production?***

another. A Portuguese with 5 bottles of wine can get 1 more bolt if they go to England. An Englishman with 1 bolt of cloth gets twice as many bottles of wine by going to Portugal.

	Bottles of Wine	Bolt of Cloth
England	-7	+3
Portugal	+10	-2
Total	3 more bottles of wine	1 more bolt of cloth

In this example, 21 working days shifted from wine to cloth production in England and10 working days shifted from cloth to wine in Portugal. The example shows that nations will be better off if they specialize in the items that cost them less to produce and exchanging them other nations. By specializing in production and exchanging products, nations can produce and consume more goods at lower cost.

inattention	독점	threaten	흐름
rarely	드물게	flow	해치다
monopoly	강압	aid	원조
coercion	무관심	harm	압력을 가하다

3.6 Critiques of the Liberal Perspective

Realists criticize liberals for their inattention to power and claim that powerful states gain more of the benefits of exchange. Realists argue that exchange is rarely free and equal. Instead, monopoly and coercion will lead to unequal exchange. Powerful states can also threaten to reduce the flow of trade, aid, and capital to harm weaker states.

unconcerned	착취	mislead	제국주의
distributional	분배	reap	속이다
legitimize	무관심	prosperity	이익을 본다
exploitation	정당화하다	imperialism	번영

Marxists criticize Liberals, by claiming that Liberals are unconcerned about distributional issues. Marxists accuse Liberals of seeking to legitimize inequality and exploitation, and argue that liberals mislead workers into thinking they will reap the benefits of economic prosperity along with the capitalist class. Marxists claim that exploitation and imperialism are hidden within the Liberal's notion of interdependence.

environmental	진보	redistribution	요약하자면
advances	따라잡다	wealth	재분배
scarcer	고갈되다	in summary	판단
catch up	환경	judge	부

- ***Which nation has a comparative advantage in wine production?***
- ***Which nation has a comparative advantage in cloth production?***

Marxists also argue that technology cannot solve the world's economic and environmental problems. Despite technological advances, Marxists point out that resources are becoming scarcer, which is leading to a more zero sum world. Technology could also lead to increasing inequality, since technology is based on the rich countries advantage in knowledge. Marxists insist that poor nations will have difficulty to catch up. Problems of exploitation, underdevelopment and poverty can only be solved through redistribution of wealth to poor nations.

So, to summarize, this chapter defined two different types of theories: normative and positive, discussed the definition of a theory and provided a method by which to judge a theory's utility. This chapter examined Liberalism, discussing the meaning and basic assumptions of Liberalism and why it is important in I.P.E., and reviewed the three strands of Liberalism, and the Liberal positions on trade and development and the role of the state. This chapter also explored the logic of orthodox Liberalism, including the concepts of Comparative Advantage and Absolute Advantage, and the Realist and Marxist critiques of Liberalism.

- ***What is the Realist critique of liberalism?***
- ***What is the Marxist critique of liberalism?***

Chapter

4 Realism

This chapter explains why Realism is important in I.P.E., reviews the economic and non-economic versions of Realism along with Realism's basic principles, and describes the Realist approach to economic development.

school of thought	펠로 폰 네소스 전쟁	Great Depression	강조하다
Peloponnesian War	대전 사이의 기간에	collapse	대공황
dominant	학파	emphasize	붕괴되다
interwar period	지배적	refer	참조하다

Realism is the oldest school of thought in International Relations, beginning with Thucydides (471 to 400 BC) who as the first Realist writer, wrote the first important work on International Relations – The History of the Peloponnesian War, about a war between the Greek city-states. Realism later became dominant during the interwar period. After Liberal philosophy was criticized and blamed for causing the Great Depression and the collapse of world trade, Realism rose to become the most influential school affecting views of American foreign policy leaders after World War II.

Within IPE, however, Realism remained less important than Liberalism.

The Realist emphasis on power, leads them to focus on security, rather than economics, and Realists primarily refer to politics and history in their work, not economics.

MNC	구하다	systematically	국가 중심
maintain	다국적기업	framework	제안
procure	근원	proposition	체계적으로
source	유지하다	state-centric	가정

Realists in fact, regarded the IMF and economic trade issues as "low politics," and as such did not consider these topics worthy of their attention. American Realists primarily focused on the Soviet Union. In 1970s and 1980s, though, Realists again became interested in I.P.E., and Realist Robert Gilpen started to examine the power of American multinational corporations (MNCs). In the 1970s and 1980s Realists demanded inclusion of the study of the state in I.P.E.

• ***How did Realism become the dominant I.R. theory?***

4.1 Two Strains of Realism

Of the two strains of Realism, the first school neglects economics. This school developed from the ideas of Niccolo Machiavelli, an Italian philosopher and diplomat, who lived from 1469 to 1527.

Machiavelli wrote the classic, 'The Prince,' which provided leaders advice on gaining and maintaining power. Machiavelli said that power was more important than wealth. According to Machiavelli: "Gold will not procure good soldiers, but good soldiers will always procure gold."

The second school developed out of the ideas of Thucydides and the Mercantilists, providing a Realist approach to I.P.E. Thucydides considered wealth an important source of military strength, and Mercantilists systematically linked wealth with power. The Mercantalists wrote from the 16th to the 19th centuries, calling for foreign policies which would increase their country's gold reserves.

• ***What is the Realist view of economics vs. politics?***

4.2 Basic Tenets of the Realist Perspective

The Realist framework is summarized in three propositions: Realists assume the state is a Rational Unitary Actor in Anarchy, or R.U.A. States are the most important actors. This is known as the state-centric assumption.

anarchy	비국가
downgrade	이익 단체
non-state	무정부 상태
interest groups	중요하지 않다고 생각하다

overestimate	자조 체계
context	없는
lacking	과대 평가하다
self-help system	속에서

Realists downgrade the importance of sub-national or non-state actors, like interest groups and M.N.C.s and argue that Liberals overestimate importance of MNCs, institutions and groups. Realists assume that states act as rational individuals in pursuing the national interest. This is referred to as the unitary rational-actor assumption. Realists also assume that states act in the context of an international system lacking central government. This final assumption is known as the anarchy assumption.

- ***Why did Machiavelli think that power was more important than wealth?***
- ***How should states get gold? Do Realists support free trade?***
- ***What is a RUA?***

4.3 Motives of the Actor in Realism

Realists emphasize that the rules of the international system create anarchy. In the international system there exists no central authority above the nation state and no central authority to enforce rules. So, International Relations, therefore is a self-help system for states, in which each state must look after its own interests, rely on itself and avoid dependence on others.

sovereignty	자율적	authority	통상적으로 하지 않는 일을
whatever	주권	struggle	투쟁
autonomous	에 대하여 책임지지 않다	otherwise do	그 자체
answer to	자기가 원하는 것	itself	권위

What do states want according to Realists? States want to preserve their national sovereignty. Sovereignty here means that a government has the right to do whatever it wants within its own territory. States are separate, are autonomous, and answer to no higher authority, due to anarchy. States then, pursue power in order to preserve sovereignty. Hans Morgenthau, the most important Realist writer after World War II encapsulated this view when he remarked that "International Relations, like all politics, is the struggle for power."

- ***Why do Realists assume states are the actor?***
- ***What is anarchy?***
- ***How do Realists think states act in anarchy?***

4.4 The Definition of Power

"Power" is defined as state A's ability to get state B to do something it would not otherwise do. Power is not only influence itself, but also the ability or potential to influence others.

capabilities	군사의	diplomatic	특정
military	무형	draw on	외교
element	능력	long term	사용하다
intangible	요소	particular	장기간

4.5 The Elements of Power: Power Capabilities and Power Resources

A nation's power capabilities allow it to exercise influence in the short term. Among power capabilities, Realists tend to see military force as the most important element of national power in the short term. Intangible elements, however, like the national will, diplomatic skill, and popular support for the government can also influence capabilities. Power resources, on the other hand, are elements that an actor can draw on over the long term to develop particular capabilities.

- ***According to Realists, what do states want? Why?***
- ***What is power and how do you measure it?***

GDP
territory
geography
natural resources

천연 자원
지리학
국내총생산
영토

shape
measure
protect
surpass

지표
모양
능가하다
보호하다

Gross Domestic Product (GDP), population, territory, geography, and natural resources are power resources. Power resources only change slowly and they shape an actor's potential power. The best single measure of a state's power may be its GDP, which combines size, technological level, and wealth.

4.6 The Nature of International Relations According to Realism

Because all states seek to protect their sovereignty, most Realists believe that cooperation is difficult to attain under anarchy. In the Realist view, states most care about their relative position. Each state's attempt to surpass the others will block cooperation.

security dilemma
bolster
insecurity
armaments

강화하다
안보의 고민
군비
불안정

purposes
offensive
arms race
worse off

더 불행하다
공격적
목적
군비 경쟁

- ***What are power capabilities and resources?***

What results is the Security Dilemma. When each state seeks to bolster its own security, it increases the insecurity of other states. Building up armaments for defensive purposes, for instance, looks offensive to neighbors. This cycle leads to an arms race in which all are worse off.

concentrate	집중	serve their interest	강조하다
absolute gain	세계 무역 기구	neutral	그들의 이익을 증진하다
WTO	설립하다	prescriptions	처방전
craft	절대 이득	stress	중립적인

Liberals, in contrast, concentrate more on absolute gains, and are unconcerned about the gains or losses of other states. Realists, though, see economic relations as a zero sum game. One side's win means that the other side has lost. In contrast to Liberals, Realists also think that international institutions, like IMF, World Bank and World Trade Organization (WTO), are crafted by powerful states to serve their own interests. International institutions are not neutral promoters of cooperation as liberals believe.

The economic policy prescriptions that follow from the standard Realist view stress the need for protectionist policies

---

- ***What is the Security dilemma?***
- ***How do Realists view international organizations?***

vulnerability	산업 정책	committed to	세계화
selective	취약성	capitalism	자본주의
industrial policy	전략적인	globalization	탁월한
strategic	선별적	preeminent	옹호하다

that limit the vulnerability that comes with economic exchange and specialization. They also stress the need for selective government interventions in the form of industrial policy aimed at developing certain sectors of the economy considered to be 'strategic.' The Marxist critique of Realist economic policy is that Realists remain committed to capitalism.

Realists prefer politics and states over economics. Realists also ask whether globalization and interdependence are increasing. In the Realist view, globalization, if it is increasing, is due to states wanting it to increase, not to technology or advances in communication, as Liberals would argue. Powerful states can stop globalization if they desire to do so, regardless of levels of technology.

4.7 Realism and Development

Realists view industrialization as a requirement to gain

- ***What is the problem with free trade according to Realists?***
- ***How do Realists view globalization?***

national security and military power. Two preeminent Realist thinkers, Alexander Hamilton in the U.S. and Friedrich List in Germany, specifically argued for industrialization.

treasury	독립 전쟁	base	숙련 된 노동
subject	주제	encourage	장려해야 하다
manufactures	재무부	skilled labor	시행하다
revolutionary	제조업	implement	기반

American Alexander Hamilton (1755-1804) served as U.S. Secretary of the Treasury. Hiss 1791 "Report on the Subject of Manufactures" argued in favor of economic protectionism for economic nationalism. Hamilton sought to strengthen the U.S. economy and promote economic development in order to obtain national independence and security. Hamilton was particularly concerned by the fact that the U.S. was unable to supply its own military during the American Revolutionary War.

To build an industrial base, he argued that the government should encourage introduction of foreign technology, capital, and skilled labor. The government should implement

protectionist	공무원	branch	수학
civil servant	장벽	mathematics	흥정
barriers	게임 이론	predicting	종류
game theory	보호 주의자	bargaining	예측

• ***What policy do Realists support for economic development?***

protectionist trade policies, like tariffs, to raise the domestic cost of protected protects in order to aid domestic manufacturers.

The second famous Realist thinker, Friedrich List (1789-1846), was a German civil servant, professor and politician influenced by Hamilton. List also argued for trade barriers to promote manufacturing and maintained that the education system was also important for promoting economic development.

4.8 Realism and Game Theory

Game theory can be used to show the effects of anarchy and relative gain motivations on cooperation. Game theory is a branch of mathematics concerned with predicting bargaining outcomes.

setting	상황	a set	추론하다
alternative	행동	payoffs	그것에 해당하는
moves	반복해서	aims	결과물
repeatedly	대안적	deduce	목적을 둔 것이다

In game theory a 'game' can be thought of as a setting in which players choose among alternative moves, either once

- ***What is game theory?***
- ***Why do scholars use game theory?***

or repeatedly. Each combination of moves, by all the players, results in a set of payoffs to each player. Game theory aims to deduce likely

outcome	무엇인가를
given	우리가 알고 있을 때
open to them	결과
prisoner	죄수

dilemma	의심하다
trespassing	무단 침입
suspect	고민
robbery	강도

outcomes, given the player's preferences and the possible moves open to them. Games are defined by the number of players and the structure of the payoffs. Realists maintain that anarchy makes cooperation difficult to achieve. We can understand there logic through the prisoner's dilemma game.

4.9 The Prisoner's Dilemma (PD) Game

In the PD game, police arrest two people (person A and person B) for trespassing. Police suspect that A and B also committed robbery,

confession	배반
cells	고백
defect	감방
conviction	유죄선고

prison	배신하다
betray	감옥
imprisonment	보내다
reason	이유

but, police are unable to prove that robbery was committed

without a confession from person A or B. The police put A and B into different prison cells where they are unable to communicate with one other. The police then separately question and interrogate each prisoner. A and B can cooperate with one another by not confessing to robbery. A and B can defect, though, by confessing to the robbery. Their score will depend on their decision. The number in the top right represents A's score. The number in the bottom left represents B's score. Police tell person A that his conviction for trespassing is certain. If A and B say nothing to the police and cooperate with one another, they will both spend one year in prison. If A says that they committed the robbery and B says nothing, A will receive a favor from the police and will go free. B though, will receive 10 years in prison. If both A and B defect and betray one another, they will both receive a reduced sentence of 5 years in prison. If A does not betray B, but B betrays A, A will receive 10 years imprisonment, while B goes free.

This game has a single solution, which is that both prisoners will confess to the police and betray one another. Each prisoner will reason as follows:

insight	가하다
impose	피할 수 없는
forgo	통찰력
inevitable	가하지 않다

realistic	협력적인
contexts	문맥
sustained	현실적인
cooperative	오랜

"If my partner is going to confess, then I should confess

too, because I will get a slightly shorter sentence that way. If my partner is not going to confess, then I should still confess because I will go free that way instead of serving a short sentence." In each situation, defection yields the greater individual reward.

The other prisoner follows the same reasoning. The dilemma is that by following their individually rational choices both prisoners will end up serving a fairly long sentence. They could have achieved the collectively shortest penalties by cooperating with one another and keeping their mouths shut. But since they act to maximize their individual interest, they are unable to attain the collectively best outcome. In I.R., the P.D. game has been used to gain insight into trade politics.

Consider the decisions of China and the U.S. about whether to impose economic sanctions, or raise tariffs on one another. The best outcome would be that one's country but not

The the other raises import tariffs. The second best would be for neither side to raise tariffs on the other side; the third best would be for both nations to impose tariffs on the other. The very worst outcome is to forgo economic tariffs on the

---

- ***Why is the Prisoner's Dilemma game a dilemma?***
- ***Why can't the prisoners in the Prisoner's Dilemma game cooperate?***
- ***How is the prisoner's dilemma game similar to the international system?***

other country while the other country imposes them on our country. Each state's leader reasons as follow: "If they impose economic sanctions by raising tariffs, we must too, and if they don't, we still should." The model predicts an inevitable China-U.S. trade war, even though both states would be better off avoiding one.

The PD model can be made more realistic by allowing the players to play the game repeatedly. In most I.R. contexts, the same actors will bargain over the same issue repeatedly over a sustained time period. A strategy of reciprocity after a first cooperative move

bring about	상호
mutual	가능해집니다
tit for tat	받는 만큼 되돌려 주기
reciprocity	상호주의

provoke	명성
cheating	속임수가
reputation	정직
honesty	유발하다

can bring about mutual cooperation in a repeated Prisoner's Dilemma game. This strategy is called Tit for Tat. Game theorists have shown that in a repeated PD game, the possibility of reciprocity can make it rational to cooperate. The other player realizes that any defection will provoke a defection in response. A reciprocal strategy thus helps to trains the other actor to cooperate.

Liberals argue that international institutions can promote

- ***What is a Tit for Tat strategy? Does it lead to cooperation?***

cooperation by increasing transparency. Everyone will know what everyone else is doing, so cheating will become more costly. States can develop reputations for honesty and states can identify cheaters.

identify	식별하다	roots	착취
transparency	투명성	uneven	허용하다
dependency	의존	permit	뿌리
World Systems	세계 체제	exploitation	고르지 않은

This will allow states to cooperate with honest states and punish cheaters. Transparency thus makes a reciprocal strategy much more effective.

- ***How do institutions and reputation make cooperation in the prisoner's dilemma more likely?***

Chapter

5 Marxism / Structural Theory

This chapter explores the major assumptions and principles of Marxist class theory. All major varieties of Marxism (Marxism, Imperialism and Dependency) predicted the end of capitalism, and while they've so far all been proven incorrect, Marxist theory remains very relevant to explain inequality and exploitation.

Marxism includes several different approaches: Marxism, Dependency Theory, World Systems Theory and Gramscian analysis. Each of these approaches has roots in Marxism. Marxism is also sometimes called Structuralism because it refers to an uneven social structure, which permits exploitation.

bourgeoisie	자본가 계급	order	모드
proletariat	요인	mode	질서
subordinate	종속된	feudalism	비 생산
factor	최하층계급	non-producing	봉건 제도

Marxists see a history of exploitation, with the capitalist class, known as the bourgeoisie, exploiting the working class, referred to as the proletariat.

5.1 The Basic Tenets of the Marxist Perspective

Like Realists, Marxists see economic relations as zero sum and conflictual. They take the opposite view of the Realists regarding the relationship between politics and economics, however. For Marxists, politics is subordinate to economics, and economic power trumps political power. The relationship among classes is the main factor affecting political order. In the Marxist view, each mode of production (feudalism and capitalism) is characterized by two opposing classes (an exploiting non-producing class, and an exploited class of producers).

temporary	자율성
autonomy	균형이 잡힌
balanced	반영
reflect	일시적인

social welfare	사회 복지
instance	필요악
evolution	예
necessary evil	진화

- ***What do Marxists think is more important, Politics or Economics?***
- ***Can the state be autonomous from classes? Why or why not?***

Marxists view the state as merely a tool of the dominant class, which in capitalism is the bourgeoisie. The state, they insist, can only possess temporary autonomy from classes. This can occur only temporarily in unusual situations, when classes are equally balanced in power, such as immediately prior to social revolution. States policies thus reflect the interests of the dominant, capitalist class. Marxists insist that even social welfare policy is an instance of states acting in the long term interests of capitalism.

5.2 The Evolution of Marxism

While highlighting the human misery caused by capitalism, Marx concluded that capitalism was a necessary evil.

asiatic	잉여
self-sufficient	공동체들
communities	아시아
surplus	자급 자족

convert	임금
invest	변환
lead to	투자하다
wages	양산

Capitalism would help societies develop out of what he called the 'Asiatic mode of production' found in India and China, where growth was stifled and the economy consisted

---

- ***Does capitalism have no purpose according to Marxists?***
- ***What were Marx's three problems in capitalist societies?***

of small self-sufficient village communities. Under capitalism, private business owners would take surplus from workers, convert it into capital, and invest it in new business, increasing the amount of capital. In this process, though, the non-producing capitalists exploited the producing class of workers. Marx predicted that this unequal economic exchange would lead to three problems in capitalist societies: low wages, under-consumption, over-savings and over-production.

poverty	노동자 계급	transition	전환
working class	붕괴되다	Socialism	사회주의
downturn	빈곤	Communism	살아남다
collapse	침체	survival	공산주의

The working class also comprised the great majority of consumers. So, by reducing wages, capitalists would also reduce consumption. Karl Marx and Friedrich Engels thus predicted that the poverty of the working class and surplus production, would lead to falling consumption, an economic downturn, the collapse of capitalism, and ultimately to the transition to socialism, and then communism. Of course, the problem with this prediction was that capitalism survived.

5.3 Imperialism

Vladimir Lenin provided a solution, explaining that the existence of imperialism was able to explain capitalism's continued survival.

colonies	원료	manufactured goods	신식민지주의
raw materials	식민지	competition	경쟁
agriculture	농업	Neocolonialism	제조품
markets	시장	intellectuals	지식인

Colonies fulfilled a role critical to capitalism's survival by providing raw materials and inexpensive agriculture to rich states as well as markets for surplus capital and manufactured goods.Workers in industrialized countries were able to survive, thanks to the cheap food imported from the colonies. Imperialism then, according to Lenin, allowed capitalism to forestall and postpone a worker's revolution. But, Lenin also argued that the supply of colonies was limited, and competition for colonies would eventually lead to the end of capitalism. Once again, however, these predictions proved to be incorrect as capitalism survived the transition from imperialism to independent states.

- ***How did Lenin's Theory of Imperialism try to solve the three problems?***

5.4 Dependency Theorists

Marxists responded by developing new approaches: Neocolonialism and Dependency theory. Dependency theory in fact emerged as the dominant approach to development among Latin American intellectuals in the 1960s.

core	주변	industrialization	산업화
periphery	제 3 세계	commission	무역의 조건
at the expense	희생으로	process	위원회
third world	핵심	terms of trade	과정

Development scholars explained that capitalists in advanced capitalist countries, alternatively known as the core, or the North, dominated and exploited poor states in the periphery. Dependency theorists argued that capitalist development in advanced countries of the north came at the expense of the third world's (also known as the periphery or South) autonomous industrialization and development.

Dependency scholar Raul Prebisch, Director of the U.N. Economic Commission for Latin America explained the process through which the advanced industrialized nations exploited the third world: through declining terms of trade. Terms of trade refer to the prices of goods which nation's purchase and sell from the rest of the world - the prices of exports and imports.

• ***What is the core and the periphery?***

primary	1차	primary products	일정한
commodities	수요	constant	1차 생산품
finished advanced goods	고급 완성품	trapped	갇혀
demand	상품	underdevelopment	저개발

The relative prices of goods produced by third world countries (primary commodities) was falling, as rising incomes in the advanced countries led to higher demand for finished advanced goods. Demand for primary products was constant, however, leading their relative price to fall. As the living standards of citizens of industrialized countries rose, they purchased nicer automobiles and high technology intensive goods, but not many more primary products. As the relative price of developing country exports fell, they found that they were trapped in underdevelopment.

import	개발	industrial sector	투입
substitution	제한하다	infant industry	국제수지
developed	대체	balance of payments	유치산업
restrict	수입	input	산업 부문

5.5 Import Substitution Industrialization (ISI)

Dependency scholars thus concluded that the only way for poor countries to develop was to cut ties with developed core. Their governments should restrict imports from the core in advanced industrial sectors. The resulting higher prices would provide an incentive for local infant industries to develop. Industrialization would help the poor countries escape from poverty and exploitation. Several of the Latin American Least Developed Countries (LDCs) adopted the dependency scholar's ISI policies in the 1950s and 1960s. Protection of basic industries, like textiles largely succeeded. But ISI failed to promote the development of more advanced industries, like auto manufacturing. The countries that implemented ISI suffered from balance of payments troubles. They were importing more than they exported, which drained their foreign currency reserves. Part of the problem was that these ISI nations continued to import capital inputs like auto parts for their protected infant industrial sectors.

uncompetitive	경쟁력 없는	machinery	무시하다
lack	신흥 공업국가	ignore	인프라
necessary	필요한	insufficient	불충분
NICs	부족한	infrastructure	기계

Their new industries were very uncompetitive, however and lacked necessary skilled labor. The protected market into which they were selling wasn't large enough, since most LDC consumers were poor and lacked much consumer power.

- ***How does declining terms of trade keep poor countries underdeveloped?***

The prices of industrial products were so high they couldn't be exported or compete on the international market. ISI had failed to help LDCs develop.

In the 1980s, a group of countries known as the 'NICs' or Newly Industrial Countries (Korea, Taiwan, and Brazil) experienced rapid economic development. This fact led some Dependency scholars, like Fernando Henrique Cardoso, to revise Dependency theory and argue that a type of development was possible. But Dependency scholars insisted that this new type of 'Dependent Development' was limited. Under Dependent Development wages remained low, technology development was limited, and the NICs still remained dependent on imports of capital, machinery and technology from the advanced countries.

- ***How would ISI promote development?***
- ***Why did ISI fail in Latin America?***
- ***Why did ISI succeed for basic industries like textiles but fail for advanced industries like automobiles?***

5.6 Critiques of Dependency Theory

Numerous critics attacked the Dependency argument. Scholars argued that the concept of dependency was difficult to measure. Dependency theorists also ignored the many domestic causes of LDC economic difficulties, such as insufficient capital markets, inefficient infrastructure, and weak property rights. The market could not properly function without secure property rights, access to loans, and expensive transportation and transactions costs.

integration	예측 된	relevant	미묘한
predicted	개방된	persistence	관련된
triumph	승리	nuanced	드문
openness	통합	rare	지속성

Critics also argued that Dependency theory was wrong about the relationship between integration to the world economy and growth. The successful development cases of export oriented Korea, Taiwan, and China demonstrated that integration promoted economic growth.

Marxists, Imperialists, Dependency scholars had all predicted the end of capitalism, but capitalism hasn't disappeared and instead some LDCs became NICs and developed. Communist Soviet Union collapsed and both Chinese and the Russians

---

• ***What is Cardoso's 'dependent development'?***

adopted capitalism. Since the 1980s, LDCs have largely adopted liberal, capitalist reforms. They've moved away from nationalism, protectionism, ISI, and state socialism towards privatization, trade and capital openness and markets. Does this represent the triumph of liberalism over Marxism? Not necessarily. Aspects of Marxist theory are still relevant today. Marxist theories show the prevalent inequality and exploitation that exists in the system. Other strands of Marxism account for capitalism's continued persistence.

5.7 World Systems Theory

This more nuanced Dependency approach is from Immanuel Wallerstein, who argued that development is possible, but rare.

buy off	우방국가화	prevent	종속된
loyalty	분할과 통치의 (각개격파)	revolution	혁명
divide and rule	줄이다	subordinate	식별
lessen	충성	identify	방지

Development only happens when the advanced nations buy off the loyalty of a few select developing countries. The industrialized nations use a divide and rule strategy,

---

• ***What were the criticisms of Dependency Theory?***

making alliances with a few development countries to lessens opposition from the LDCs and prevent revolution.

5.8 Gramscian Theory

Gramscian cultural ideological theory also explains capitalism's ability to survive. Antonio Gramsci was the former leader of Italian Communist Party. He argued that capitalists used ideology and culture to gain the support of subordinate groups and prevent revolution. Due to ideological beliefs, like the 'American Dream' workers did not identify as workers, but instead viewed themselves as future capitalists. Workers therefore believed that their exploitation and suffering were only temporary conditions before their eventual success as entrepreneurs, which weakened their

willing	해당되는	typically	촉진하다
contribute	공헌	promote	대체적으로
applicable	도구	disagreement	이야기 하다
tools	기꺼이	address	의견 차이

willingness to contribute to a worker-led rebellion. So in summary, while the predictions of Marxism, Imperialism and Dependency theory about capitalism's death were wrong, inequality and exploitation remain. Marxist views are still applicable to explain that. The Marxist use of economic class to analyze society is also widely applied in Political Science and in International Relations.

- ***Which Marxist predictions were incorrect?***
- ***What is World Systems Theory?***
- ***According to Antonio Gramsci, how did capitalists maintain power?***
- ***Which useful analytical tools were provided by the Marxist perspective?***

Part II

Trade Policy

Chapter

6 The Tools of Trade Policy

This chapter examines the tools of trade policy and explains why trade policy is important. Trade policy is typically considered as a prime tool of economic development and can be used to promote development. Scholars disagree over the role of trade policy in development, however, and disagree over the right types of trade policy. This chapter does not address those questions,

foundations	관세
tariffs	목적
quotas	기초
objectives	할당량

exports	자율 수출규제
shelter	장벽
barriers	피난처
V.E.R.	수출

but instead examines the foundations of trade policy today. It is important to understand, though, why scholars are so concerned about trade policy. We can see examples of trade policy throughout the world. The governments of every country in the world, other than one, are involved in managing their country's trade. Hong Kong comes the closest in the world to a country with perfectly free trade. Hong Kong has no tariffs or quotas. Every other country,

There are two main objectives of trade policy: protection and exports. Protection in this case refers to shelter for domestic firms against imports. States also use trade policy to promote or support export competitiveness. Trade changes the relative prices within an economy, which can threaten domestic producers.

Before discussing different political explanations for trade policy let's examine the most important instruments and tools used by nations to control trade. There are two categories of trade policy tools: tariffs and non-tariff barriers. Non-tariff barriers, or NTBs include: quotas, voluntary export restraints (VER),

subsidies	기준	foreign exchange	제한
purchases	빨간 테이프	restrictions	코드
red tape	보조금	taxes	외환
standards	구매	code	세금

subsidies, government purchases, red tape, standards and

- ***Which country does not use trade policy tools?***
- ***though, uses these main tools of trade policy.***

foreign exchange restrictions.

6.1 Tariffs

Tariffs are simply taxes on imports. Calculation of tariffs can be quite complicated however. For instance, the U.S. tariff code is so large that it encompasses five books, almost one meter thick, and this is the case for most other countries. Why is the tariff code so large?

hundred thousand	실태
status	세계 무역기구
W.T.O.	단순화하다
simplify	십만

most favored	특혜의
regional	최혜국 대우
preferential	지역
treatment	대우

The tariff rate depends on the type of product and the country of origin. There are hundreds of thousands of different categories of products and each one has a different tax rate.

Each of the countries that produce all of those products also has a different tax status. The establishment of the WTO was to simplify this problem. Under WTO rules each member state receives IWTO nation most favored status. Hypothetically, all imports of a given product should have the

---

• ***How does international trade affect domestic prices?***
• ***What are tariffs and what do they do?***

same tax rate. But the WTO also allows nations to participate in regional preferential trade agreements, which provide better trade treatment to some nations than to others. So computing a tariff requires information about the country of origin and the specific item category.

levy	하향 협상	visible	국내
fixed tax	부과	domestic	양적인
negotiated downward	고정 세	local	선명
primarily	주로	quantitative	지역

Tariffs can be levied as a percentage of the total price of each item, or as a fixed tax on each item. The advanced nations have negotiated tariffs downward, primarily because they are more visible and harder to hide from consumers.

What are the economic effects of tariffs? Implementing tariffs restricts supply and raises the domestic price of a product. Consumers lose out by having to pay a higher price. Local producers gain the higher domestic price, and the government gains tax revenue. The loss to consumers is greater than the combination of gains to the other actors however.

- ***Why is calculation of tariffs complicated?***
- ***How does the WTO deal with tariffs?***

6.2 Import Quotas

Quotas are quantitative limits on the amounts of a product that can be imported.

distort	왜곡	phase out	섬유
would look like	격차	multi-fiber	경쟁력
gap	가격	textile	다자간 섬유협정
prices	어떠할지	competitiveness	단계적으로 없에온 것입니다

Quotas distort trade, but their effect is more difficult to measure. It's hard to know what trade would look like without a quota. So, the WT.O. prefers tariffs to quotas because tariffs are more visible. With tariffs you can see the size of the gap between world prices and domestic prices and know that the gap is due to the tariff. One of the WTO's biggest free trade successes was the phase out of the multi-fiber agreement quota. The MFA was a system of textile quotas, introduced in the 1960s when advanced nations had lost competitiveness in textiles. Textiles are a labor intensive product and are politically important because textile factories provide many jobs. Advanced countries didn't want to lose their textile factories too quickly. So they limited the amount of textile imports through a system of quotas which survived for 40 years until

---

- ***What is a quota and what does it do?***
- ***Which does the WTO prefer: tariffs or quotas? Why?***

2005.

licensed	자율 규제 계약
revenue	허용된
VRA	채택하다
adopt	수익

semiconductor	생산자
price difference	가격 차이
producer	반도체
footwear	신발

What are the economic effects of quotas? Like tariffs, quotas raise the domestic price of imports. Unlike tariffs, however, quotas also give gains to licensed importers. Quotas do not provide revenue for the government.

6.3 V.R.A.s

Another type of quota is the Voluntary Restraint Agreement (VRA). The U.S. forced Japan to adopt VRAs in the late 1980 in the semiconductor and auto industries. Japanese producers agreed to limit exports to the U.S. Why would any country agree to this? Because to exporters, VRAs are better than tariffs. If a country accepts that its exports will cost more, with a tariff the price difference goes to the U.S. government as a tax. With a VRA, though, producers keep the higher price. VRAs became a barrier to trade in the steel, clothing, textiles, footwear, and automobile industries.

• ***What is a VRA?***

common	감소시키다
substantially	흔한
eliminated	상당히
vast	광대한

array	장애물
obstacles	위생
sanitary	광우병
mad cow	종류

Trade policy has undergone great changes in the last thirty years. In the 1990s it was not uncommon for countries to set tariffs up to 80% for many different products and quotas were common as well. Much of that has disappeared now. Most countries have substantially reduced tariffs and most have eliminated quotas. Other trade barriers still exist, though, such as red tape and standards. Red Tape includes a vast array of health, safety, and customs regulations, which pose obstacles to foreign suppliers.

6.4 Standards

While standards can be used to serve the public interest, they can also be used to protect domestic producers. Many WTO cases claim that sanitary standards are really trade barriers in disguise. These include WTO standard cases about chicken, mad cow beef, or wheat disease.

- ***What do exporting nations prefer to face: Tariffs or VRAs? Why?***
- ***How has trade protection changed from 2015 to 1990?***

regulations	위장	legitimate	신중
disguise	조작	scientific	합당한
genetically	규정	cautious	완전한 정보
modified	유전자	full information	과학적인

Are regulations really a disguise for protection? The E.U. has ruled that companies cannot import genetically modified grain for human consumption. Is this a legitimate health concern? The U.S. claims that this regulation lacks a scientific basis. The U.S. position is: "Show us the scientific evidence." The E.U. answers that "we can't show evidence because the issue is too new. We must be cautious until we have full information." In this complicated debate one cannot conclude that only one side is right.

certified	문제	dispute	논쟁
routine	일상적인 일	prevalent	통신
matter	공인	telecommunications	혼합
delays	지연	contract	계약

6.5 Technological Standards

Nations can also employ technological standards to protect domestic producers. China, for instance, requires that

---

- ***What is the E.U.'s policy on genetically modified food?***

every manufactured product sold in the country be certified according to its national technological standard.

While meeting a national standard should be a routine matter, in China's case there are often problems and delays. Disputes about government procurement are also common. Governments may try to purchase more expensive domestic goods instead of lower-priced foreign goods. This practice is especially prevalent in the telecommunications and construction industries and with defense contracts.

direct	원조
assistance	곧장
facing	경쟁
competition	직면

WTO	보조금을 주다
subsidize	애매
vague	신용
credit	세계 무역 기구

6.6 Export Subsidies

Export subsidies are direct government assistance to industries facing foreign competition. World Trade Organization (WTO) rules mandate that directly subsidizing an exporter is illegal. WTO rules are vaguer about government-subsidized credit, however.

EU	허용되는	agricultural	환경
airplane	유럽 연합	preserve	농업
dispute	비행기	ecology	보존하다
permitted	논쟁	farmer	농부

The U.S. and the European Union (EU) have a complicated agreement concerning subsidies to airplane exporters, which has been a continuing dispute.

6.7 Agricultural Subsidies

According to WTO rules, some subsidies are permitted, but some are not allowed. Paying farmers to preserve ecology is permitted, but paying a farmer to export is not allowed.

- ***How do countries use NTBs to protect from imports?***
- ***Which types of subsidies are allowed by the WTO and which are not allowed?***

Chapter

7 Justifications for Trade Protection

infant industries	최적	strategic	육성
job	일자리	spillover	전략적
income	유치산업	nurtured	전파
optimum	소득	free from	으로부터 자유롭게

Scholars and politicians have put forward several arguments in favor of trade protection. These include: infant industries, jobs, defense, income distribution, optimum tariffs, strategic trade, and technological spillover.

7.1 Infant Industries

One of the oldest arguments for protection is that industries

---

- ***Why do some argue to protect trade for infant industries?***

need to be nurtured and given time to grow, free from foreign competition.

capital market	제대로 작동	grow up	공공재
working properly	유익한	defense	성장
profitable	자본시장	public good	국방
private investment	민간 투자	intervention	개입

Liberals respond by arguing that if capital markets are working properly, an industry that could be profitable in the future will receive private investment. If this is not the case, a country should try to improve their capital markets. Liberals point out that protected industries will not become competitive, since they have no incentive to improve efficiency. In other words, infant industries will never grow up.

7.2 Defense

Defense is seen as a public good and government intervention is needed to provide defense.

- ***Do liberals support trade protection for infant industries? Why or why not?***
- ***Why do some argue to protect trade for defense?***

raw material	손해가 덜	supplies	물자
goods	원료	danger	남용
less costly	비축	abuse	위험
stockpile	상품	claim	청구

To ensure security a government might need to protect supplies of raw materials, goods, and weapons. There is much debate about how much protection is needed, though, and which industries should be protected. It may be less costly to stockpile supplies than to protect a domestic weapons industry. Again, there is the danger of political abuse. To receive protection, many industries will claim to be important for national security.

justifiy	노동시장	retraining	풍부한
labor market	낙농	abundant	재교육
steel	정당화	scarce	미숙련 노동
dairy	강철	unskilled labor	희소한

7.3 Jobs

Trade protection is defended and justified for protecting

- ***Is defense a good argument for protection?***
- ***Why do some argue to protect trade for preserving jobs?***
- ***Do liberals support trade protection for jobs? Why or why not?***

the jobs of workers in industries that compete with imports. Labor markets rarely work perfectly, so workers who lose jobs through foreign competition often cannot quickly find new jobs. But jobs that are lost through trade should be compared to the jobs gained through trade. And jobs that are maintained through protection are costly. The annual cost to U.S. consumers of saving a job in the steel or dairy industries is $1 million per job. One job protected in the auto industry costs $160,000. It would be less costly for governments to spend money on assistance to workers that lose jobs and on worker retraining programs.

7.4 Income Distribution

In nations in which capital is abundant and labor scarce, labor, particularly unskilled labor, loses through trade. Thus, trade could increase income inequality in rich countries.

superiority	주요
key	우위
integrated	집적
circuits	회로

flat	판표시장치
panel display	규모의 경제
alternative	평면
economies of scale	대체

7.5 Strategic Trade

Strategic trade policy became popular in the U.S. in the late 1980s. Scholars argued that Japan was developing technology superiority in certain key industries. So, the U.S. needed to protect and develop those key industries. These industries included integrated circuits and flat panel displays. Alternative energy technology is another strategic industry. Strategic industries often have economies of scale, with high fixed costs of production.

entry	높은 이익	chicken	좁은
desirable	게임 이론	narrow	1 차선
profit margin	진입	one lane	침로를 벗어나는
game theory	가치있는	swerve away	치킨

The high cost of entry means few producers in the world market. Few producers means that there will be low competition and this leads to higher prices and higher profits. Government financial support can encourage growth of desirable industries with high profit margins.

Game theory can capture the competition between nations over the location of strategic industries. This is the chicken game in which there are two players. Each player is driving a

---

• ***Why do poor citizens in advanced industrial countries lose through trade?***

car. Both are driving down a narrow, one lane road. The first driver to swerve away

yield	똑바로 가고	prefer	충돌
neither	치명적인	tie	납득시키다
catastrophic	양보	crash	선호하다
stay straight	둘 다 아니다	convince	무승부

yields the road to the other driver. If neither driver swerves, the result is a catastrophic accident.

The best individual outcome for each driver is to stay straight while the other swerves. A crash is the worst outcome for both players. Each player would prefer to win over tying, prefer to tie over losing, and prefer to lose over crashing.

down the road	위협	empty threat	결과
accomplish	할수있다	constrain	공허한 협박
threats	이해	steering wheel	핸들
interpreted	도로를 계속	outcome	제한

What is your strategy in this case? You would want to convince the other side that you were committed to driving down the road. This could be accomplished through threats. But threats would be useless if they are interpreted as empty

---

- ***What is the strategic trade argument for protection?***
- ***What is the chicken game?***
- ***Why is strategic trade like the chicken game?***

threats. Taking action to constrain one's actions could help. Like throwing the steering wheel out the car window. Threats can become more credible if alternates are no longer possible. This chicken game is similar to a strategic trade case in which two nations that would like to produce in a strategic industry, such as airplanes. Each nation would like to be the only producer, since the market is only large enough for one producer. Without competition, the sole producer would be able to sell airplanes at a high price. The worst outcome for both is if both nations produce. That would mean losses for both sides, since the market is too small for two producers. Government intervention can give one side an advantage.

one side	전념
committed	순서
logic	한쪽
order	논리

unique	독특한
head start	이점
first mover	맨 먼저 움직이는 사람
advantage	유리한 출발

It sends the signal that one side is deeply committed to producing. If the U.S. government subsidizes its producer Boeing, then Airbus might decide not to enter the industry. Trade protection and export promotion can thus be justified on strategic trade theory logic.

- ***How do you win the chicken game?***
- ***Why does airplane manufacturing have economies of scale? Why?***

	Don't Produce	Produce
Don't Produce	0,0	100,0
Produce	0,100	-5,-5

So the order of preferences in this case is: DC〉CC〉CD〉DD. There is no unique outcome to this game. The firm with the head start (the first mover) can gain the advantage. The other nation will see that the industry is already occupied and abandon production.

7.6 Technology and Knowledge Spillovers

Certain industries can possess positive "externalities" or "spillovers,"

positive	흐름	employee	양성
externality	보상	train	존재하다
compensation	외부효과	innovation	혁신
flow	긍정적인	exist	직원

which benefit others without compensation. Knowledge can flow between firms in the same industry. Ideas about new products and new ways to produce goods are exchanged from

---

- ***What is a technological spillover?***
- ***Are technological spillovers a good reason for trade protection?***

employee to employee. Firms in industries with spillovers may train workers who can be employed by other firms. Spillovers can lead to innovations key to new products and improved production methods. Knowledge spillovers are said to exist in aircraft, computers,

electronics	의도적으로	facility	휘발유
pharmaceutical	연구 개발	shipbuilding	조선
intentionally	제약	gasoline	시설
research and development	전자 제품	engines	엔진

electronics, and pharmaceuticals. Spillovers explain why many semiconductor firms intentionally located research and development facilities to Silicon Valley. The film industry is located in Hollywood in Los Angeles, California. But ideas can also spread between different industries, too.Scholars argue that the American auto industry developed in Detroit in the 1890s because of the local shipbuilding industry.

Firms shifted from building gasoline engines for ship to building them for automobiles.

optimum tariff	제품	reviewed	부분
force down	강제 하향 조절	actual	시행하다
revenue	최적 관세	implement	살펴보다
product	수입	section	실제

Proponents claim that governments should aid and protect industries with externalities and encourage them to locate in the domestic economy.

7.7 Optimum Tariff Theory

Optimum tariffs are only possible in very unusual situations. Optimum tariffs are only effective if a country's market is really large. In this case, if the country reduces consumption, it could lower the world price of the good it consumes. A tax on imports could reduce worldwide demand and force down the price. So a tariff would allow consumers to pay less and the government to gain tax revenue. But few country's consumption is large enough to influence the world price of a product.

- ***What is the optimum tariff theory for protection?***

8 Three I.R. Theoretical Approaches to Trade

9 Societal Theories of Trade

10 Institutional Theories of Trade Policy

11 An International Theory of Trade Policy: Hegemonic Stability

12 Testing Different Theories through the Corn Laws

Part III

Theoretical Perspectives on Trade

Chapter

8 Three I.R. Theoretical Approaches to Trade

The first part of this book has examined the various different tools of trade policy, such as quotas and tariffs and reviewed trade protectionism, including strategic trade policy and technology externalities. This section of the book will examine the factors that determine the actual trade policies that nations implement, and consider different theories of trade policy.

emotional	주제	natural order	평화
topic	정하다	peace	자연 질서
Christian	감정적	conflict	논란이 많다
ordain	기독교도	controversial	분쟁

- ***Why is trade policy politics usually more controversial than monetary policy politics?***
- ***Is trade policy becoming more or less important?***

Trade relations have been an emotional topic for societies from early times. Early Christian philosophers argued that God had ordained trade. Trade was considered as part of the natural order. Seventeenth century world peace theory linked free trade with peace. On the other hand, trade conflict was common in Europe from the Middle Ages. Trade is controversial because groups see

welfare	통화	religious	종교적인
monetary	재정	industrial states	최빈개도국
financial	환경 주의자	LDC	다국적기업
environmentalist	복지	MNC	공업국

their welfare directly affected by trade policy. It's more difficult, on the other hand, to see a connections to monetary, investment or financial policy. Business, labor, farmers, consumers, environmentalists, cultural and religious group all have preferences over trade.

Trade relations have been strongly affected by globalization. From 1985 to 1997, trade to GDP rose from 16.6% to 24% in the industrial states and 22% to 38% in the Least Developed Countries (LDC)s. Average trade to GDP rose to 30% per cent in 2014.

A growing share of trade is taking place within multinational corporations (MNC)s and

affiliates	글로벌가치사슬	benefit	비교 우위
GVCs	양의 합계 게임	justify	이득
positive sum game	상호	specialize	전문화하다
mutual	계열사	comparative advantage	정당화하다

their affiliates. Trade between M.N.C. affiliates, within global value chains (GVCs) accounts for so 80% of global trade. As a result, trade is now increasingly linked with investment.

8.1 The Liberal View on Trade

Liberals seek to promote free trade. They view trade as a positive sum game providing mutual benefits to all states. Adam Smith and David Ricardo provide theories to justify free trade. Smith showed how absolute advantage produces gains from free trade. All states benefit if they specialize in the goods they produce best, and then trade with each other. Ricardo's theory of comparative advantage

cheaply	싸게	textiles	받는
opportunity cost	부문	earn	보상하다
sectors	규제	winner	우승자
restraints	기회 비용	compensate	직물

• ***What is the Liberal view of free trade?***

demonstrated that even countries that cannot produce a good more cheaply than others can gain through trade. Comparative advantage exists in cases where one country can produce an item at a lower cost, in terms of opportunity cost, than another country. Every nation possesses its own comparative advantage, and thus all nations gain through trade.

Liberals point out that the costs of trade protection are very expensive. In the case of the U.S. in the 1990s, consumer losses in the 11 sectors of the U.S. economy with the highest tariffs equaled $2.3 billion per year. Export restraints in textiles cost consumers more than $21 billion. The U.S. government earned about $1.4 billion in revenue through tariffs. Every job that was saved through protection cost the average U.S. consumer $170,000 per year. Liberals argue that free trade increases overall economic efficiency. While some may lose from free trade, the winners can compensate the losers, so that everyone can still gain.

8.2 Marxist Opposition to Free Trade

Marxist	얼어	in place	이웃나라
division of labor	마르크스 주의자	value added	부가가치
consequence	분담	gain	체재하다
frozen	결과	neighbor	이익

Marxists oppose free trade and argue that the division of labor through trade can have serious political and economic consequences. Division of labor occurs when different parts of a manufacturing process take place in different countries. Some states, particularly LDCs, can enter into the international division of labor engaging in low value added production and stay frozen in place. They become specialists in unprofitable production. So, trade doesn't benefit all countries equally. Marxists argue that it's better to be at the top of the international division of labor than to be at the bottom and better to specialize in high value added production.

• ***What is the Marxist view of free trade?***

8.3 Realist Argue Against Free Trade

The Realist argument against free trade begins with the assumption that states pursue relative gain, not absolute gain. States worry about their neighbor's gain if they trade.

pursue	보호주의	international system	이익 단체
prisoner	죄수	objectives	요구
dilemma	추구하다	interest group	국제체계
protectionism	고민	demands	목적

The Realist's ideal policy is for a state to protect its market, while other states pursue free trade. The Realists think about trade in terms of a prisoner's dilemma game. In the end, all nations will defect and pursue protectionism.

Scholars also categorize the factors that determine trade policies into international systemic factors and domestic factors. The next chapter will examine the importance of domestic theories of trade.

- ***What is the Realist view of free trade?***

Chapter

9 Societal Theories of Trade

Societal theories of trade policy argue that a government's trade policy objectives are formed by the demands of societal interest groups.

liberalize	사회적인	point out	의류
high technology	서비스	distribution	분배
service	첨단 기술	income	지적
societal	자유화하다	apparel	소득

Politicians design and implement policy in response to the demands of groups. So, for example, the E.U. resists liberalizing imports of agriculture due to the demands of European farmers. The U.S. wants to open foreign markets to U.S. high technology and service exports because of the demands of U.S. interest groups. Societal theories point out that trade can affect the domestic distribution of income. Some groups will gain income through trade and other groups will lose income through trade. In the case of the U.S., textile and apparel factories have closed because of imports.

employ	압력	liberalize	제조업체
pharmaceutical	임금	manufacturer	영향
wages	고용	Find out	알아내다
Pressure	제약	impact	자유화

When factories, closed, thousands of workers in those industries lost their jobs. On the other hand, those employed in the pharmaceutical industry and financial sector in the U.S. have increased their wages through exports. As one might expect, financial service firms have pressured the U.S. government to liberalize world trade, while textile manufacturers have exerted pressure to reduce textile imports. So, to understand and predict trade policy one must look at the interests of groups and determine which groups prefer trade protectionism and which groups prefer liberalization.

9.1 Group trade policy preferences

The first step in this process is to find out trade's impact on the income of individuals.

predict	행동
collective	집단
action	로비
lobby	예측하다

like-minded	관련된
relevant	생산 요소
factors of production	산업 부문
industrial sector	뜻을 함께 하는

Societal level theories predict that if trade increases an individual's income, they should favor trade. If trade decreases an individual's income they should favor protectionism.

9.2 Collective Action

After determining whether people prefer free trade or not, the next step is to determine whether they will lobby together with other like-minded people for their preferred policy. This chapter examines two different theories about group trade preferences. There is disagreement about identifying the form of the relevant societal interest group. Some types of interest groups more easily overcome barriers to collective political action.

One theory assumes that the important societal groups are economic classes. This approach is termed the "factors of production theory." The other theory which assumes that

---

- ***Which two elements are needed for political groups to take action?***
- ***Which two types of societal groups take political action?***

industry groups are most important is called the "industrial sector theory."

redistribute	요소	argue	이론
factor	재분배	determine	의존
production	모델	rely	주장
model	생산	theorem	결정

While both theories agree that trade policy redistributes income, they disagree over the type of groups affected by trade policy.

9.3 The Factors of Production Theory

The factor model argues that the factors of production determine a country's trade policies. This theory relies on the Heckscher-Ohlin model. In the 1920s and 1930s two liberal Swedish economists, Eli Hecksher and Bertil Ohlin developed this theorem to explain comparative advantage.

endowment	제품	LDC	반면에
product	선진국	on the other hand	가난한
more advanced	자본이 풍부한	poor	최빈개도국
capital rich	부존	tend	경향이 있다

According to Heckscher and Ohlin, there are three factors of production: land, labor, and capital. A nation's endowment in these three factors determines the cost of products produced in each nation. More advanced economies are capital rich. LDCs (least developed countries), on the other hand, are poor in capital and rich in labor. Some countries, like Canada, for instance, tend to have a lot of land.

absolute	와 다른 한 가지	relative	인구
amount	절대적인	population	평방 킬로미터
ratio	비율	square km	상대적인
to another	양	labor scarce	노동력이 희소한

An abundant factor of production is not determined by a country's absolute amount of land, capital, or labor, however. Factor abundance is determined by the ratio of one factor to another, relative to other countries. For example, the U.S. has a larger population than Korea: 300 million to 50 million. But the U.S. also has more than six times as much land as Korea (about 100 times): 9,372,610 square km vs. 99,392 square km. So, compared to Korea, U.S. is land abundant and labor scarce. Korea is land scarce and labor abundant.

comparative	비교적	wheat	가축
abundance	곡물	cattle	자본
land-intensive	풍부	wealthy nations	밀
grain	토지 집약적	capital	선진국들

- ***What is the Hecksher Ohlin Trade Theory?***
- ***What are the three factors of production?***

Nations with comparative abundance in land, like the U.S. or Canada, would have the lowest cost of producing land-intensive products, which require much land to produce, such as grain (wheat) or cattle. Advanced, wealthy nations have a relative abundance of capital, and would have the lowest costs of producing capital intensive goods, such as railways, airlines, telecommunications, chemical factories, electrical power plants.

capital-intensive	철도	chemical factory	발전소
railways	자본 집약적	power plant	공급
airlines	항공사	supply	화학 공장
telecommunications	통신	cheap	싼

LDCs have an abundant supply of cheap labor. LDCs are defined as nations below $1,000 GDP per capita. By definition they have very little capital per citizen

textiles	호텔 산업	economist	경제학자
toys	장난감	built on to	선호
hotel industry	섬유	favor	이득
export	수출	benefit	보충

LDCs possess the lowest costs of producing labor-intensive goods, such as textiles, toys, and the hotel industry. Through trade each nation should export its lowest cost products, which will be in its most abundant factor of production.

• ***How can we determine an abundant factor of production?***

9.31 The Stolper - Samuelson Theory

In the 1940s, two U.S. economists, Wolfgang Stolper and Paul Samuelson, built onto the H.O. theory. They tried to explain why some groups within a given country favored free trade while other groups favored protectionism. Stolper and Samuelson argued that free trade benefits

owner	희소한 요소를 가진	capitalist	셔츠
poorly endowed	희소한	magnification	확대
scarce	소유자	imagine	상상하다
lose	잃다	shirts	자본가

the owners of the abundant factor and hurts owners of the poorly endowed factor. Owners of abundant factors would gain from free trade, while owners of scarce factors would lose through free trade, and instead favor protection. In a state like the U.S., free trade would benefit capitalists. American capitalists should favor free trade. In a state like China, on the other hand, free trade would benefit workers. Chinese workers should favor free trade.

• ***What is the abundant factor in LDCs? How do you know?***

9.32 The Magnification Effect

Here is an example to show how this process works. Imagine that there are only two countries, the U.S. and China, and they produce only two products, shirts and computers, using only two factors: labor and capital.

computer	수요
relatively	줄입니다
demand	컴퓨터
falls	상대적으로

firms	적어지다
manufacture	청산하다
fewer	제조
liquidate	회사들

Computers are capital intensive and shirts are labor intensive. The U.S. is capital rich and labor poor whereas China is labor rich and capital poor. Capital will be relatively cheap and labor relatively expensive in the U.S., and labor is relatively cheap and capital relatively expensive in China. So, the U.S. will export capital intensive goods (computers) and import labor intensive goods (shirts). And China will export labor-intensive goods (shirts) and import capital-intensive goods (computers).

This is how trade affects the prices for labor and capital. As demand for U.S. shirts falls, U.S. firms manufacture fewer shirts. U.S. shirt producers liquidate the capital in their American shirt factories

---

- ***What is the Stolper and Samuelson Model? Which factor favors free trade?***

fire	동시에	buy	양도하다
at the same time	생산	release	불균형
expand	해고	imbalance	흡수하다
production	확대	absorb	사다

and fire American shirt workers.

At the same time U.S. computer firms are expanding production, as Chinese buy more American computers. As U.S. computer production expands, American computer firms need more capital and labor. They need to build new factories and hire new workers. At the same time, the American shirt industry is releasing workers and capital.

But there is an imbalance between the amount of labor and capital released from the shirt industry and the amount absorbed into the computer industry.

bankrupt	많은	high demand	가격
plenty	파산한	price	이자율
not much	많지 않다	wages	임금
few	많지 않다	interest rate	높은 수요

American shirt firms were labor intensive. As they go bankrupt, they release plenty of workers, and not much capital.

• ***Why does free trade lead to increased wages in China and lower wages in the U.S.?***

American computer producers are capital intensive. They hire a few workers and need plenty of capital. So in America, there are more workers than needed, and capital is in high demand. In America, high demand leads the price of capital to rise, while low demand leads the price of labor to fall. This process is called the magnification effect.

9.33 The China-U.S. Trade Policy Example

What is the price of labor? It is wages. What is the price of capital? It is the interest rate.

cost	빌다	direction	인상
borrow	비용	contract	계약
dynamic	현상	rise	여분의
opposite	반대로	extra	방향

The interest rate is the cost of borrowing someone's capital. So, in the U.S., wages fall and the interest rate rises. This same dynamic takes place in China, but in the opposite direction.

As the Chinese computer industry contracts it releases lots of capital, but few workers. The Chinese shirt industry expands, demanding many workers, but using little capital. Excess demand for labor leads Chinese wages to rise, and extra capital leads the interest rate to fall.

- ***What is the magnification effect?***
- ***What is the price of capital?***

both	희소한
scarce	양국
lose	지속된
uninterrupted	잃다

equalize	따라
minimize	분할되다
according	똑같아 지다
divide	최소화

So in both countries, trade leads the income of the scarce factor to fall, and increases the income of the abundant factor. Abundant U.S. capital and abundant Chinese labor both gain from trade. Scarce U.S. labor and scarce Chinese capital both lose. If trade continues uninterrupted, factor incomes in the U.S. and China will equalize. Eventually the wage and interest rates will be the same. So, Sameulson and Stolper argued that the scarce factor wants to minimize trade and the abundant factor wants to expand it. In the US, workers (as the scarce factor), want protection, while in developing countries, labor (as the abundant factor) wants free trade, and capital wants protection. According to this theory, society should be divided by factor or class.

conflict	역사적인
famous	유명한
historical	예
example	충돌

aristocratic	곡물조령
battle	곡물 시장
Corn Law	전투
grain market	귀족

Workers, capitalists and farmers should always be in conflict over trade. In fact, there are some famous historical examples of class conflict over trade. For example, in the 1800s in England, aristocratic landowners battled against workers and the owners of manufacturing firms over the Corn Laws, which had protected the domestic grain market.

Who would have been the scarce and abundant factors in England in the 1800s? Who would be in favor of protection of the grain market and who would have been opposed?

landowner	예측하다	align	특정
oppose	반대하다	particular	증거
implement	지주	evidence	제휴
predict	시행하다	closely	긴밀히

Workers and owners favored free trade, while landowners opposed it. Labor and capital were relatively abundant while land was scarce. The workers and owners won and England became the first nation to implement a free trade policy. This class theory of trade politics would predict that political parties would align themselves with particular economic classes. There is some evidence of this in advanced nations. "Labor" parties are closely aligned with workers.

Democratic Party	제조자	AFL	노동 조합
Republican	민주당	CIO	산업별 조합회의
represent	공화당	labor union	미국 노동 총연맹
manufacturer	대표하다	prominent	저명한

- ***What will happen to the price of capital and labor in China and the U.S. if trade continues uninterrupted?***

In America in the 1800s, the Democratic Party was supported by farmers, while the Republicans represented manufacturers and workers. In numerous instances, economic classes have taken a position on trade policy according to the Stolper Samuelson Theory. In the U.S., the A.F.L. C.I.O., (American Federation of Labor and Congress of Industrial Organizations) a federation of 64 labor unions representing 13 million U.S. workers, has been a prominent

N.A.F.T.A.	기업인 간담회	intra-industry	흐름
Business Roundtable	북미 자유 무역 협정	flow	에 따르면
C.E.O.	최고 경영자	according to	산업 내
N.A.M.	전미제조업자협회	resource intensive	자원 집약적

critic of globalization. The A.F.L. C.I.O. was critical of N.A.F.T.A. As the theory would predict businesses have also been supportive of free trade. The U.S. Business Roundtable, a business association comprised of the CEOs of the largest U.S. corporations, strongly supports globalization. The National Association of Manufacturers (NAM), representing 14,000 U.S. manufacturing firms, also supported free trade.

- ***Who favored the Corn Laws in England? Why?***
- ***What is American labor's preference on trade policy, according to Stolper Samuelson?***

9.34 Critiques of Hecksher - Ohlin Trade Theory: Intra-Industry Trade

Most of world trade flowed according to comparative advantage and the Hecksher Ohlin theory in the early period of globalization in the late 1800s and early 1900s. England exported capital and skill intensive manufactured goods, while importing land and resource intensive products from developing countries.

composition	특히	autos	변동이 없어지다
modern	현대	one another	교환
especially	구성	level out	서로
intra-industry	산업 내	exchange	자동차

The Hecksher Ohlin theory can also explain the composition of trade between advanced nations and poor nations today, in which advanced nations export capital-intensive manufactured good and import labor-intensive imports from developing countries. Most of modern trade cannot be explained by Hecksher Ohlin Theory, however, especially the large amount of trade between the advanced nations, which all have cheap capital and expensive labor. With similar factor endowments, according to the theory, these nations would have little incentive to trade with one another.

The Hecksher Ohlin theory especially fails to explain or

- ***What is American labor's trade preference according to Stolper Samuelson?***

account for intra-industry trade, in which products are traded within the same industry group. In this type of trade, both sides export and import within the same industry. Intra-industry trade is most likely within industries that are the abundant factor within their nation. For example, the US, Japan and Germany all produce autos and trade them with one another.

After World War II, intra-industry trade grew very rapidly from 1950s to 2000, before it leveled out. Up to 60% of U.S. trade and 60% of European trade is intra-industry trade. Germany and France have the largest intra-industry trade ratios. They exchange similar, but not identical, products.

consumer	대해 생각하다	taste	전문화하다
care about	차별화	variety	다양성
differentiation	소비자	specialize	취향
satisfy	만족시키다	sophisticate	정교한

- ***How much of world trade can be explained by the Hecksher Ohlin model?***
- ***What is intra industry trade (IIT)?***
- ***Can Hecksher Ohlin explain intra industry trade (IIT)?***

9.4 The Reasons for Intra-industry Trade

9.41 Consumer Taste

Consumer taste can account for some of the trade within industries. Most consumers also care about product differentiation and intra-industry trade satisfies consumer tastes for variety. Intra-industry trade expands the size of the market, allowing for production of more specialized and sophisticated products. The automobile industry, for instance, has much intra-industry trade.

interchangeable	규모의 경제	similar	경쟁력있는
for instance	기능	endowment	유사
function	예를 들어	perfectly	완벽하게
Economies of Scale	교환할 수 있는	competitive	부존

Most consumers do not consider autos to be perfectly interchangeable. Consumers consider German cars to be different from American cars. A Mercedes is different from a Kia, for instance. Each type of car possesses a somewhat different and unique function.

9.42 Economies of Scale

Economies of scale provide another reason for trade between nations with similar factor endowments. Economies of scale exist when the per unit price of production declines with the scale of production. Markets for some goods are not perfectly competitive. In other words, high costs prevent new firms from entering these industries.

production costs	착수	research and development	조립 라인
per unit	생산비	testing	모형
initial	단위당	prototype	연구 개발
start-up	초기	assembly line	실험

In the automobile industry, for instance, the production costs per unit decreases as the size of production increases. The price of the first car produced can be five times higher than the cost of the 10,000th car produced. The price differential results from large initial start-up costs in research and development, developing and testing prototypes, and the costs to build a factory and arrange the assembly line. Start-up costs need only be paid once. Once a factory is constructed it can be used for decades.

limit	억제하다	serve	전체
inhibit	후발 진입자	entire	공급
late entrant	제한	particular	적당한
be able to	할 수 있다	correct	특별한

So unit costs decline with increased production. The existence of economies of scale in some industries limits the

---

- ***How do Consumer Tastes lead to intra industry trade (IIT)?***
- ***What are economies of scale?***

number of firms able to produce and inhibits late entrants to the industry. In some industries, only a few firms may be able to serve the entire world market. There is no particular reason where producers are located among the many countries with the correct factor endowments.

have to pay	확실히 자리를 잡은	encourage	촉진
established	에 의해 결정된다	not necessarily	집중된
is determined by	생산 규모	be better off	더 나은 것입니다
scale of production	지불해야 한다	concentrated	반드시 그런 것은 아닙니다

A late entrant would have to pay much higher costs than established firms, and not all prospective firms are able to pay the high costs of entry. So, firm location is determined by history in addition to resource factor endowment. An industry with economies of scale is located where it first reached an efficient scale of production. This tends to be the nation where the product was first produced. By expanding the size of the market, trade also tends to encourage economies of scale. This is not necessarily a bad thing. We should all be better off if production is concentrated where there is the lowest cost.

- ***How do Economies of Scale lead to intra industry trade (IIT)?***

in the long run	빨리	compete	수송
competitive position	경쟁적 입지	identical	동일한
get up to	장기적으로는	transportation	경쟁하다
fast enough	할 수 있을 만큼	incorporated	이뤄지는 것

Airplanes are as cheap as they are because Boeing and Airbus produce them efficiently.

Perhaps in the long run we'd be better off if planes were manufactured in China and Brazil, but firms in these nations can't gain a competitive position. They have been unable to get up to a large scale fast enough to compete. So intra-industry trade occurs in the airplane sector when Europeans and Americans export and import them to one another. Their location is an accident of history.

9.43 M.N.C. Networks

Multinational corporation networks are another type of intra industry trade, although in this case, the trade does not exactly involve the exchange of identical products. Instead, related products within the same industry are transported from one country to the other as they move through a global production network. The different stages of producing a product are not incorporated within one factory.

each stage	나뉘어져	principles	명백한
sliced up	위치	obvious	특정
location	와 같은	hardware	원칙
in line with	각 단계	certain	하드웨어

Instead, each stage is sliced up and moved to a new location. Typically the movement to a new location is in line with principles of comparative advantage. The industry for which this process is most obvious is electronics hardware, or information technology (I.T.) hardware. The different stages of I.T. hardware production have very different factor intensities.

Certain stages of the production process,

integrated circuit	입력	packaging	양
fabrication	제조	immediately	포장
demand	집적회로	enormous	엄청난
inputs	필요	amount	즉시

like integrated circuit fabrication, are extremely capital intensive and demand high science and technology inputs. Another stage, which is very labor intensive, such as packaging and testing of integrated circuits will immediately follow. Then, there will be another capital intensive and high technology stage, followed again by other labor-intensive assembly stages. So the electronics hardware global production network creates an enormous amount of trade.

CPU	시설
ship	중앙 처리 장치
facility	배
circuit board	회로 기판

component	노트북
laptop	넘나들다
cross	장비
border	경계

For example, consider Intel's production of central processors. Most of Intel's factories are in the U.S. The central processing unit (C.P.U.) is produced in the US and is then shipped to Costa Rica which has a large packaging and testing facility. The C.P.U. is then shipped to Asia to be attached to a circuit board. Then it is shipped to China for sub-assembly, and then shipped out for additional high tech components. Finally the C.P.U. is shipped back to China to be assembled into a laptop. Virtually all laptops are final assembled in China. In the end, the C.P.U. has crossed sevem international borders. This type of exchange looks like intra industry trade.

record	자료처리기
commodity	상품
sub-assembly	기록
data processing	하위 부품을 조립

transaction	거래
network	네트워크
successive	강도
intensity	연이

Most of these transactions are recorded as the same commodity: subassemblies for a data processing machine. In fact, though, each transaction is a different stage in a

---

• ***What is a MNC network?***

production network, and each successive activity has a very different factor intensity.

MNC	듭니다	location	복제하다
structure	단계	intensive	곳에
place	다국적기업	replicate	패턴
stage	구조	pattern	집약적으로

So when M.N.C.s structure the whole production process, they intentionally place each individual stage in a location where the intensively used factor is abundant. Labor intensive production is carried out in labor abundant developing countries and capital intensive production takes place in industrial countries. So, global production networks tend to replicate a pattern of trade

consistent	지휘 하에 있다	branch	조립
carry out	지점	sales outlet	판매 매장
conduct	일치하는	part	부품
branch	수행하다	assembly	지점

which is consistent with comparative advantage. Much of world trade is carried out within M.N.C.s: 80% of trade takes place in 'value chains' linked to M.N.Cs. A value chain is the process by which a company adds value to a product. The highest percentage of U.S. M.N.C. trade (75% of total trade) is between the U.S. and Japan and Ireland. Why?

For Japan, much of the trade between the U.S. and Japan is

in autos. Most trade is conducted by large Japanese companies, which own manufacturing branches or sales outlets in the US. For instance, Toyota imports parts from Japan for assembly in the US.

base	여러	access	장
several	고등 교육을 받은	attractive	접근
speaking	회화	site	매력적인
highly educated	기지	information technology	정보 기술

Ireland, on the other hand, serves as a base for U.S. M.N.C.s. Ireland has several advantages including low taxes, speaking English, a highly educated population, and access to the E.U. Ireland is an attractive investment site, especially for U.S. M.N.C.s interested in information technology.

affiliates	계열사	outsource	일치
bring back	수출	accord with	수명주기
remain	간단한	lifecycle	위탁하다
less sophisticated	남아있다	cutting edge	첨단 기술이

U.S. companies use their affiliates to bring goods back to the U.S. from Ireland. Each of the main regions of the global economy has regional global production networks. In autos

---

- ***How do MNC networks lead to intra industry trade (IIT)?***
- ***Why do MNCs like Intel build international networks?***
- ***Why do MNCs divide up the different parts of the production process and place them in different countries?***

there is N.A.F.T.A., which includes auto production networks in Canada, the U.S. and Mexico. In Europe, German auto firms have expanded auto production into Eastern Europe. The highest value added and skill intensive stages remain in Germany, where labor is expensive, while less costly, less sophisticated stages are located in Poland and Slovakia. In East Asia, Japanese auto firms outsource parts to China. These production networks accord with comparative advantage.

9.44 The Product Lifecycle

The product lifecycle model provides another explanation for intra-industry trade. When a product is first developed and is cutting edge and sophisticated, it is produced in an advanced country. Research and development is capital intensive and thus takes place in industrial countries where the price of capital is relatively low.

mature	이동
routine	동남
moved out	일상적이
S.E.	성숙

versions	대량 생산
mass produce	버전
general	최근
recent times	일반

Production costs are high due to steep startup costs, so the product is sold at a high price in industrial countries. The

- ***Why is so much of U.S. M.N.C. trade between the U.S. and Japan and Ireland?***

product is highly profitable due to the absence of competition. Over time a variety of the product becomes mature. Its production becomes more routine and does not require as much capital as before. Labor becomes a larger component of cost and production is moved out to developing nations, like China and S.E. Asia, where labor is cheaper.

So, advanced nations produce high technology versions of a product, while developing nations mass produce the basic, cheaper version. Intra-industry trade is created when advanced and developing nations exchange different versions of the same product.

9.5 The Sectors Model of Trade Policy

9.51 General Problems with the Factors Model of Trade Policy

According to the factors model, then, we would expect that changes of political party, which are aligned with distinct classes, would lead to changes in national trade policy. In recent times, though, this has become difficult to find.

- ***According to the Product Lifecycle, where are products first developed and where are mature goods produced? Why?***
- ***How does the Product Lifecycle lead to intra industry trade (IIT)?***

coalition	소프트웨어 제작자	identical	동일
steel producer	철강 생산자	substitute	취급 되다
software maker	연합	categorize	분류하다
criticism	비판	be treated	대체

Class coalitions have been divided over trade policy. For instance, among U.S. manufacturers, steel producers prefer protectionism, while software makers prefer free trade.

9.52 Criticism of the Assumption of Factor Mobility

A couple of theoretical problems dog (trouble) the factors model. One problem is that the factors model assumes that all workers are identical, and possess identical skills. The model contains the unreasonable assumption that workers can costlessly substitute for one another. A solution to this problem, then, is to categorize labor into different groups according to skill: lower skilled workers and higher skilled workers. Each group can thus be treated as a

distinct	강력히	correlate	연관성이 있음
low skilled	설문 조사	view	유동성
survey	명백	oppose	반대하다
strongly	미숙련	mobility	견해

distinct factor of production. According to this new revised model, trade still reduces the incomes of low skilled workers in the U.S., where low skilled workers are a scarce factor of production. Trade would raise the incomes of highly skilled workers, however, which are an abundant factor in industrial countries like the U.S.

In fact, survey data shows that in the US, income level strongly correlates with views towards trade. Those with over $50,000 income per year, which are more likely to be skilled workers, are much more favorable towards free trade. Those with incomes under $50,000, which are more likely to be unskilled, more strongly oppose free trade. The factors model also contains the problematic assumption of complete mobility within factors of production. A alternative model, known as the sectors model, challenges this assumption.

costless	이동	stuck	아마
shift	재교육을 하다	spinning machine	거래하다
retrain	비용이없는	presumably	갇혀있어
distant	먼	transaction	방적기

9.53 When Factors are not Mobile

In reality factors of production are not fully mobile. Capital and workers do not costlessly move from one industry in to another one. For instance, the factors model assumes that capital employed in the textile industry can easily and quickly be shifted into the computer industry. It also assumes that workers in textiles manufacturing can seamlessly shift into computer production. But this certainly is not true.

A textile worker cannot simply begin to produce computers.

They will first need to receive costly retraining. They may also have to move to a distant region, to a place without a social support network of family and friends. Many workers will resist such a move. Capital used to make textiles is stuck in that industry, and can't move to computers. What is the use of a spinning machine in the computer industry? Presumably one could sell the spinning machine, and use it to purchase machines for a computer factory. But the transaction would be costly, since one would be selling a spinning machine into a market with little demand for the machine. One could sell a used machine to a manufacturer in China, but there would be transport costs, and transaction costs as well. So much of the value of the spinning machine would be lost.

divide	자본에 대한 수익이	vacant	고생
sector	소득	suited	변환
return to capital	부문	convert	빈
income	분열시키다	suffer	적합합니다

Therefore, the sectors model argues that trade politics is affected by competition between industries. Trade politics does not divide society between classes. Trade politics instead

---

- ***How can trade affect skilled workers and non-skilled workers differently?***
- ***In the U.S., who is more likely to support free trade? Skilled workers or non-skilled workers? Why?***

divides society along industrial sectors. When tariffs are raised, in some industries wages and the return to capital (or profits) will rise together. In other industries, wages and the return to capital will fall together. Trade politics makes workers and capitalists in one industry oppose workers and capitalists in another industry. Workers and capitalists in the same industry become allies.

The previous example of the U.S.-China trade of shirts and computers looks very different under the sectors model. As with the factors model, the imports of shirts to the U.S.

would lead to less shirt production in the U.S. Shirt factories would close and shirt workers would be fired and go unemployed, losing income. Unlike the factors model, under the sectors model shirt businessmen would also lose income. Why? Because capital cannot move. Businessmen in the shirt industry would be unable to move their capital into the computer industry.

In the U.S., one can easily see instances of abandoned capital in bankrupt, uncompetitive industries. Bankrupt steel factories in Pennsylvania stay vacant for decades, since the building is suited for only one use – making steel. A steel

---

- ***Are workers perfectly mobile between industries? Why or why not?***
- ***Is capital perfectly mobile between industries? Why or why not?***

factory can't easily be converted to some other use. The assets are lost. So, in our example, both shirt workers and business owners suffer from trade.

predict	경쟁	apparel	섬유
competition	생물 기술	textiles	미국 섬유 제조 협회
bio-technology	예측하다	footwear	의류
oriented	지향적	ATMI	신발

The same process holds true in the computer industry. Workers and capitalists in computers both gain. The effect on workers is different from the prediction of the factors model, though. The factor model predicted that computer workers would lose income. In that model, computer workers would face competition from all of the unemployed workers released from the textile industry and their wages would fall.

But the sectors model argues that computer worker's incomes are safe from competition, so their wages rise. The unemployed textile workers cannot enter the computer industry and take their jobs. So, the greater demand for computers leads to higher wages for computer workers too, and both computer workers and owners gain from trade. So, industries that use the abundant factor gain from trade, while industries that use the scarce factor lose from trade.

In advanced nations, industries that use capital intensive

• ***What is the Sectors Model of trade politics?***

and high technology gain through trade. These industries include computers, aircraft, software, pharmaceuticals, and bio-technology. These industries are called the 'export oriented' sector. Industries that use the scarce factor are called the 'import competing' sector. In advanced countries firms in the import competing sector are in labor intensive industries like apparel, textiles, and footwear.

There is also evidence of import competing sectors opposing export oriented sectors. For instance, the American Textile Manufacturers Institute (ATMI) opposed free trade agreements with South Korea and Singapore, and trade with China.

ITIC	선호
collective action	집단 행동
preferences	자동적으로
automatically	정보 기술 산업 협의회

necessary	요구
demands	합리적
organize	필요한
rational	조직화

Business associations representing U.S. high technology firms, like the Information Technology Industry Council, (ITIC) supported trade with China, and N.A.F.T.A. Another important factor which can affect which groups take political action is called the collective action problem.

- ***What is the export oriented sector and import competing sector?***

9.54 The Collective Action Problem

The preferences of individuals are not automatically transformed into political action. Collective action is necessary to turn individual preferences into political demands. Individuals with the same preference must organize to influence policy making, and organizing though can be difficult. Organizing can be so difficult in fact that groups with common interests may not organize at all. For most this is unexpected. If people are rational, why can't people with

common	이해	impede	공헌
interest	협력	public good	동기
join forces	로비	contribute	방해하다
lobby	공통	incentive	공공재

a common interest join forces to lobby for their desired policy?

Two factors impede the organization of groups: non-excludability and the costs of organizing.

9.55 Non-Excludability

Collective action can be considered as a public good, for which everyone in the group gains. In such case, it doesn't matter if someone contributed or did not contribute to the effort to attain the objective, they will receive the gain. If

---

- ***What is the collective action problem?***

someone gets a gain without contributing, does that person possess an incentive to contribute?

therefore	비용을 부담하다	punish	사전에
free riding	무임 승차	monitor	확인
rely	따라서	make sure	처벌
bear costs	의존하다	beforehand	감시

No, the incentive is to try to obtain the gain for free. Everyone can therefore be expected to attempt to gain for free, a phenomenon which is called 'free riding.' A free rider relies on others to bear the costs of a program from which he or she benefits. If everyone has an incentive to be a free rider, no one will contribute and the group will never take action. How can one overcome the collective action problem? One can try to punish those who do not contribute.

9.56 The Cost of Organizing

Free riding is related to the second problem impeding the organization of groups, which is the costs of organizing. If each member must be monitored to make sure they contributed to group goals, large groups will have a problem. Closely watching each member of a large group is very costly.

- ***What is non-excludability?***
- ***What is a public good?***
- ***What is a free rider?***

We must also remember that no one in the group knows beforehand whether or not the group will achieve its goal.

fail	확인하다	prominent	공영 라디오 방송국
amount	실패	NPR	청취자
share	양	listener	저명한
confirm	몫	bias	편견

In smaller groups each member's contribution is more important. Each member knows that if they do not contribute, it is very likely that the group will fail to achieve its goal. In larger groups, though, each member's individual contribution is less important to reaching the goal. Each person in a large group thinks – "My contribution does not matter. I may get the good even if I don't contribute. Or I may not get the good, even if I contribute." In large groups there is little connection between contributing and receiving and so there is much less incentive to contribute.

A third barrier for large groups is the size of each individual's share. The amount which ach person gains may depend on the size of the group. In a large group, the collective good must be divided among more people. So each individual gets less. Each person therefore has a weaker incentive to take political action.

So the collective action problem depends on the size of the group. In a large group, each individual contribution is a very small part of the total contribution, so there is less of a relation between giving and receiving. And the share which each individual receives is smaller, so the incentive not to give is greater. The incentive to free ride is greater. Finally, it is more difficult to confirm who has contributed in a large group.

In small group, individuals are more likely to believe that the group needs their contribution to succeed. The individual's share of the gain is also larger. And in a small group it is easier to confirm if members have contributed, so free riding is less of a problem in small groups. We can conclude then, that the collective action principle allows small groups to become more powerful than large ones.

U.S. National Public Radio (NPR) stations are a prominent example of the collective action problem. NPR stations rely on contributions from listeners and businesses for 87% of their budget, yet 80% of NPR listeners have never contributed. They are free riders. NPR stations urge individual listeners to act by claiming that they will be unable to continue operations without contributions, yet the minimal $100 contribution from each individual is too small to save the radio station. For each contributor there is little relation between giving and receiving. The large number of non-contributing NPR listeners also cannot be monitored or penalized by the radio station. NPR

- ***Are collective action costs higher for larger groups or small groups?***
- ***Do consumers protest for free trade? Why or why not?***

provides a small individual present to contributors in order to secure donations, partially privatizing the public good.

The collective action problem can also explain the bias that exists in favor of trade protectionism.

demonstrate	일방적으로	overcome	상호간의
unilaterally	시위	reciprocal	극복하다
liberalize	자유화하다	open up	설득력 있는
negotiate	협상하다	persuasive	개방

Tariffs give large benefits to a few firms in a protected industry. The costs of a tariff though are shared by many individuals and firms.

Consider a tariff on textiles. Would you, as a clothes consumer, demonstrate in the streets for a 300 Won discount on pair of jeans? Probably not. As the largest societal group, consumers face a very steep collective action problem. If you were a member of a smaller group of textile workers, however, you might demonstrate to keep your job.

The collective action problem also explains why governments never unilaterally liberalize trade. Instead, countries usually negotiate agreements with other countries for bilateral or multilateral trade liberalization. Why? Unilateral trade liberalization aids consumers, but consumers are too large of a group to mobilize in support of trade policy. Consumers fail to overcome the collective action problem. Reciprocal trade agreements allow export-oriented industries to gain. Export oriented industries are a smaller group, which can overcome the collective action problem more easily and is more likely to take political action. These industries will lobby politicians to open up the home market to foreign trade in order to gain from the reciprocal opening of foreign markets.

9.6 The Factors Model vs. The Sectors Model

So, considering the collective action problem, which model is more persuasive? The factors model or the sectors model? Which group is larger: classes of workers, farmers and capitalists, or groups of companies in industries?

Clearly certain industries can organize more easily than a whole societal class, such as workers.

Companies are already organized for production, and may be run by a single owner or family. Some industries, like steel or automobiles, have only a few producers. So only a few people, a very small group, could control a very important sector of the economy. The sectors model should thus be more widely applicable.

- ***Why is unilateral trade liberalization unusual?***
- ***Who faces higher collective action costs: industrial sectors or class coalitions?***

Chapter

10 Institutional Theories of Trade Policy

rules	규칙
respond to	결국
in turn	에 대해 관심을 두다
autonomy	자율성

typically	촉진
advance	국가 안보
national security	외무부
State Department	대체적으로

Institutions can affect how different groups compete over trade policy. Institutions establish rules, and rules influence how people organize Rules can determine if people organize by class, or organize by industry. Rules influence the political process and they influence who politicians respond to. This in turn determines which interest groups gain representation. Rules can also provide politicians with autonomy.

So, which trade policy do politicians and state officials typically desire? They may want to advance the national security interest and may be sensitive to the effect of trade on national security. For example, U.S. State Department officials in the Cold War era supported free trade.

prevalent	자율성	authoritarian	상무부
virtue	대표성	capture	포획
autonomy	보편화된	ITA	국제무역법원
representativeness	미덕	Commerce Department	권위주의적인

Free trade strengthened Western allies during the Cold War, and strengthened the U.S. alliance against the Soviet Union.

State officials may want to follow popular ideology and may follow prevalent ideas about the benefits of free trade vs. protectionism. Douglas Ray argued that American officials believed in the virtue of free trade, which enabled them to resist pressure for protection from industries.

What determines the autonomy of officials? The degree of representativeness can be important. In democratic government, government officials are accountable to politicians, who are, in turn, accountable to the voters. In authoritarian regimes, however, government officials may exercise more power over trade policy. For example, Moon Chung-in at Yonsei and my advisor at UCSD Stephan Haggard argued that Korean officials had great autonomy in the 1960s and 1970s.

- ***What are institutions and why do they matter in policymaking and politics?***
- ***Why do rules and electoral rules matter in politics?***

The alternative to autonomy is capture by a social group. In the US, the International Trade Administration (ITA) within the Commerce Department is known to favor protection of American manufacturers.

unfair	수가 더 많다
allowing	확장한
voters	유권자
outnumber	불공정한

electoral system	선거구
electoral district	할당
allocate	좌석
seats	선거 제도

The ITA often complains that foreign producers are practicing "unfair trade."

- ***If politicians or officials have autonomy, what type of trade policies do they like?***
- ***What determines the autonomy of officials?***

10.1 Representation

Voting rules determine who is represented. In England in the late 1800s allowing more people to vote led to free trade policies. Labor was an abundant factor in the late 1800s in England. Allowing workers to vote increased support for free trade. Worker voters outnumbered farmer voters and workers gained through trade as the abundant factor.

10.2 Electoral System Rules

Electoral rules allocate representation among the population, which can affect trade policy. Electoral rules define electoral districts and allocate seats in

legislative body	입법 기관	urban	강력한
Senate	이익 단체	overrepresent	대표를 지나치게 많이
House of Representatives	하원	agricultural	도시
interest group	상원	powerful	농업

legislative bodies which can influence the strength of agricultural groups in relation so industrial groups. One example in the U.S. are the different rules of representation in the Senate and the U.S. House of Representatives. In the U.S. House of Representatives, districts and seats are allocated according to population. States with more people receive more votes. For example, representatives from California have 12% of the seats in the House of Representatives while California has 12% of the U.S. population. Which interest groups gain through this electoral system? With population well represented, urban interests are favored. In the other legislative body, the Senate, each state receives two of 100 seats. Here, California receives only 2% of the seats. Which interest groups are overrepresented in the Senate? Agricultural companies, and farmers. States, like North Dakota, have small populations, but plenty of land. North Dakota has .2% of the U.S. population, but also has 2% of the seats in the Senate. Farming is important in North Dakota and in other states with low populations and farmers and agricultural companies have a powerful voice in the Senate. Land is an abundant factor of production in the U.S. So, the Senate is more likely than the House to favor free trade

constituency	선거구	single member district	소선거구
elect	대	chance	기회
constituency	선출된	local industry	지역 산업
vs.	선거구	narrow	좁은

- ***How did expansion of voting affect England's trade policy in the late 1800s?***

10.3 Constituency Size

Constituency size is another important institutional factor affecting representation. Constituency is the number of people who elect a representative. Small constituencies have fewer people, while large constituencies have more people. The size of the constituency can affect the power of industries vs. the power of classes. In the U.S. the House of Representatives has 450 small, single member districts. These small electoral districts can give industries more power and increase the chances of protectionism.

Groups in small districts have a strong incentive to organize in support of local industries, which strongly affect the local economy. Elected representatives from small districts will bring these narrow industry interests into Congress.

logrolling	서로 도와 줘	vote trading	하도록 합다
help each other	법안	permits	소수
pass	통과하다	minority	전반에
legislation	투표 거래	overall	투표 거래

- ***How do electoral rules effect representation in the U.S. Senate and Congress?***
- ***What is constituency size?***
- ***How can the size of the constituency affect the power of industries vs. the power of classes?***

Then logrolling is likely to happen: Logrolling occurs when representatives help each other to pass one another's legislation. Log rolling is a type of vote trading, permitting industries which may be a minority in the overall country, to band together to create a majority coalition and gain trade protection.

term	이웃한	cut down	대표
frontier days	협력하다	district	거래하다
neighboring	용어	representatives	잘라
cooperate	개척시대	make a deal	선거구

The term 'Log rolling' derives from the frontier days in America. Two neighboring families would cooperate to cut down a tree to build a new house. In legislative log rolling, district representatives trade votes. The representative of a district with a large textile factory makes a deal with

steel mill	관세	legislation	악명 높은
on their own	강철소	infamous	법안
policy	정책	Act	법안
tariff	독자적으로	ratify	비준하다

the representative of a district with a steel mill in favor of trade protection.

On their own, each district's representative is unable to

• ***What is logrolling?***

receive the policy they want, since tariffs on imports of textiles and steel are largely unpopular. If the two representatives trade votes and support with other representatives, they can form a large coalition and pass tariff legislation providing protection for both textiles and steel. This logrolling process resulted in protection through the infamous 1930 Smoot-Hawley Act. The U.S. constitution gives the Congress, comprised of the House and Senate, the power to make tax law. Tax law includes tariffs, which are taxes on imports, meaning that trade legislation must either start from, or be ratified by, Congress.

executive branch	선출하다	seek	대표
President	상대적으로	representative	의회
elect	대통령	push onto	추구한다
relatively	행정부	Congressional	강요하다

10.31 The Effect of Large Electoral Districts

Large electoral districts tend to weaken protectionist forces. As minority interest groups, industries are not very powerful in large electoral districts. The executive branch, the president, is elected from the largest of electoral district, comprising the whole country. Each industry is relatively less important as a part of the overall national economy. So, industries seeking protection are less likely to influence representatives of large electoral districts, such as the president. Unlike Congressional representatives, the president also cannot push the costs of protection onto someone else's district. There is only one presidential district, and it is the only one. So, whereas individual Congressional representatives, who receives most of the gain from protection while others pay most of the costs, the president receives little gain and pays all the costs of the protection. Historically presidents have thus strongly favored free trade.

10.4 The U.S. Shift from Protectionism to Free Trade

Constituent size influenced the U.S. change in trade policy in the 1930s from protectionism to free trade. Congressional authority over trade helped produce the Smoot Hawley tariff, in 1930. The story of the Smoot Hawley tariff illustrates how Congressional authority and logrolling led to protectionism.

manufacturer	장갑	item	대공황
watch	함께 결탁	rate	품목
glove	제조업체	push into	밀어 넣다
join together	시계	Great Depression	율

Prior to the passage of Smooth Hawley, representatives of districts with manufacturers of shoes, watches, gloves, textiles and other manufactured products joined together to form a large coalition in favor of protectionism. Smoot-Hawley raised

• ***How does logrolling affect policy making?***

tariffs on almost 20,000 items and was the second highest tariff in U.S. history with an overall tariff rate of nearly 60%. High tariffs cut imports and foreign countries responded with tariffs of their own against U.S. products, cutting trade. Deprived of foreign markets, U.S. producers lost sales, laid off workers and the U.S. economy was pushed into the Great Depression.

Democratic Party	주요	RTAA	위임
protectionist	보호 주의자	delegate	구성된
main	민주당	comprise	호혜통상협정법
promote	촉진하다	entire	전체

Earlier, the Democratic Party had blocked attempts at trade protectionist policy in 1929. But legislators used logrolling to pass Smoot Hawley through the Senate and House of Representatives in 1930.

Following the Great Depression three main institutional changes helped to shift the U.S. from protectionism back towards promoting free trade: the RTAA, fast track rules and the bureaucratic safety valve. Each of these three institutional reforms transferred power from the protectionist Congress and House of Representatives, with its small electoral districts, to the free trade supporting president, who came from a large electoral district.

- ***Why is the president more likely to favor free trade?***
- ***What was the Smoot Hawley Tariff?***

10.41 The RTAA

The first of the three reforms was the 1934 Reciprocal Trade Agreements Act (RTAA) which delegated trade authority from Congress to the president. The president had a large electoral district comprised of the entire country, and more strongly favored free trade.

coalition	추구한다	White House	법안
oriented	지향적	majority	백악관
seek	연합	legislation	대다수
labor union	노동 조합	Secretary of State	국무 장관

The RTAA, which helped to reduce U.S. tariffs, was passed by a coalition of export-oriented interests seeking trade liberalization that supported the Democratic Party. In the 1930s, the Democratic Party was supported by capital-intensive manufacturers, export-oriented agricultural interests, and labor unions, who worked in the capital intensive manufacturing sector. Democrats won the White House and majorities in the Senate and House, but still had difficulty getting free trade legislation through the Congress, due to logrolling. Cordell Hull, Secretary of State for President Franklin D. Roosevelt,

---

- ***Which three institutional changes helped the US favor free trade?***

realize	깨닫다	negotiate	기회
impediment	권위	reciprocal	상호간의
transfer	장애물	opportunity	압력
authority	양도	pressure	협상하다

realized that Congress was an impediment to free trade. So, President Roosevelt persuaded Congress to pass the Reciprocal Trade Agreements Act (RTAA) in 1934. The RTAA transferred the authority to negotiate reciprocal trade agreements with foreign governments from the Congress to the president. The act provided export oriented groups with an opportunity to organize and lobby. Exporters could pressure representatives in Congress to support free trade legislation, thus serving as a counterbalance to firms lobbying for protection.

completely	완전히	period	포괄적
give up	위임	certain	특정한
limited	포기하다	explicit	명백한
delegated	제한된	comprehensive	기간

Congress did not completely give up its power, however, and it couldn't since the constitution gave Congress authority over taxes. Congress limited presidential authority by only delegating authority for short periods of three years. Congress

---

- ***What was the RTAA?***
- ***Which groups supported the Democratic Party in 1934?***

also only allowed the president to take certain, explicit actions. As a result of the RTAA, though, the U.S. Congress has not voted for a comprehensive tariff since 1930.

policy	빠른 길	up or down	막다
fast track	정책	ratify	비준하다
prevent	개정하다	blocked	승인 이나 거부
amend	방지	renegotiate	재협상

10.42 Fast Track Policy Making Rules

Policy making rules also functioned to transfer authority over trade policy from the Congress to the president. 'Fast Track' voting rules that prevented Congress from amending trade agreements also strengthened the power of the executive. Fast Track rules were an example of 'up or down' voting rules. Although the U.S. president had the authority to negotiate trade agreements, Congress had to ratify the agreements. Congress blocked many trade agreements by amending them, adding protection for a certain industry to the agreement. The president would then be forced to renegotiate the agreement with the foreign country.

refuse	제공하다	accept	전체
provide	실패	reject	선거구
concessions	양보	entire	거부하다
fail	거절하다	constituency	수락

Often the foreign country would refuse to provide

concessions, and the agreement would fail. So, the "Fast Track" rule was introduced in the 1974 Trade Act. Fast track rules prevented the U.S. Congress from amending trade agreements negotiated by the president. The Senate had to vote to accept or reject the entire agreement. Senators were from larger constituencies than members of the House of Representatives.

favor	행정부	bureaucratic	관료적
worry about	선호할	safety valve	안전 밸브
redirected	보내다	appeal	항소
executive branch	걱정하다	Commerce Department	상무부

Senators were thus more likely to favor free trade. The fast track rule increased the negotiating power of the president with foreign countries. Foreign nations did not need to worry about renegotiating agreements. So, foreign nations were also more willing to offer concessions to the U.S.

10.43 The Bureaucratic Safety Valve

Congress also redirected lobbying industries to the executive branch. The bureaucratic safety valve helped Congress to avoid protectionist pressure. Industries seeking

---

- ***How did the RTAA affect trade policy?***
- ***What are Fast Track Rules?***
- ***Do U.S. Fast Track Rules make free trade more or less likely? Why?***

protection had to appeal to the Commerce Department, not their local Congressman.

victim	포함
unfair	불공정한
include	덤핑
dumping	피해자

subsidize	검토
examine	확인하다
evidence	증거
confirm	보조금을 주다

The Commerce Department then had to determine if the industry was a victim of unfair trade, which included dumping, or a foreign government subsidizing their local firms. The Commerce Department would examine the evidence and make a decision, and if it confirmed the evidence,

case	동의하다
investigate	케이스
agree	조사
recommend	제안

offset	미국 무역 대표
advantage	이점
agency	상쇄하다
USTR	기관

would send the case to the U.S International Trade Commission. The ITC would then investigate. If both agencies agreed that the firm was a victim of unfair trade, they would recommend that the president raise tariffs to offset the unfair advantage. Congress also created a new agency inside the president's Office called the U.S. Trade Representative (USTR)

• ***Did Fast Track Rules make foreign countries more or less likely to give concessions to the US?***

to lead U.S. trade policy.

transform	주요	grant	듣다
liberalizer	자유 주의자	authority	권한
main	변화시키다	hear	부여
institutional	기관적	request	요청

So, limiting the Congressional role in trade policy-making transformed the U.S. from a trade protectionist nation to trade liberalizer. To summarize, there were three main institutional changes which transferred power from Congress to the president: The RTAA, which gave the president the authority to negotiate trade deals. Fast Track Authority, which limited Congress to up and down votes on deals. Finally, the Commerce Department was granted authority to hear industry requests for protection.

hegemon	의견	show	두려움은
stability	여론 조사	fear	상황
opinion	패권국	situation	보여 주다
poll	안정	prefer	선호하다

- ***What was the Bureaucratic Safety Valve? How did it favor free trade policy?***
- ***Who was more likely to favor protection: Commerce Department or Congress?***

Chapter 11

An International Theory of Trade Policy: Hegemonic Stability

Previous chapters examined domestic institutional and societal theories of trade policy. This chapter explores the international explanation of trade policy, known as Hegemonic Stability Theory. A well known opinion poll demonstrates American popular attitudes about hegemony. Polls showed that Americans feared rising Chinese power. Americans were asked which situation they preferred: scenario A in which

over	간	concerned	상대적인
decade	일반 대중	relative	포기
general public	지속적으로	willing	걱정하는
consistently	10년	sacrifice	기꺼이

the U.S. economy grew at 25% over a decade while China grew at 75%, or scenario B in which the U.S. economy grew at 10% over a decade while China grew at 10%. Scenario A corresponds to a situation in which there is free trade between China and the U.S. which enables China to catch up to the U.S. but delivers faster growth to the U.S. Scenario B corresponds to U.S. trade protectionism in China trade ties, which cuts trade and reduces economic growth on both sides. Public opinion polls show that about 80% of the American general public consistently favor #2. Americans are very concerned about relative wealth and security. In fact, they are willing to sacrifice an

enormous	엄청난	single	자유주의
absolute	주장하다	dominant	단일
indicate	나타나다	liberal	지배적
claim	절대적인	order.	질서

enormous increase in absolute wealth. The poll indicates American's fear of a rising hegemonic challenger.

Hegemonic stability theory claims that an open, stable international economic system is produced by a single, dominant or hegemonic state. This hegemon possesses a large share of world resources, and is able to provide leadership. The hegemon is also willing to create a liberal economic order.

- ***Do Americans care about hegemony?***
- ***What is a hegemon?***

necessary condition	지배적	collapse	의지가 없다
study	연구	unable	붕괴되다
dominant	필요한 조건	unwilling	할 수 없는
leadership	지도력	maintain	유지하다

The hegemon is a necessary condition for an open or stable international economy.

Political Scientist Charles Kindleberger is the creator of hegemonic stability theory. In Kindleberger's study of the Great Depression he discovered the importance of a dominant state in providing world economic leadership. Kindleberger wanted to understand the cause of the collapse of the world economy after 1929 and found that the U.K. was unable and the U.S. was unwilling to maintain

interwar	인식하다	avert	막다
recognize	책임	crisis	발휘
responsibilities	패권국	exercise	다음과 같은 방법
hegemon	양 대전 사이	following way	위기

an open and stable world economy during the interwar crisis. While the U.K sacrificed economic growth and exports in order to provide the world economy with an overvalued British pound to serve as an international currency, the U.K. was no longer the world's leading power. The British possessed the will, but not the might. The U.S., on the other hand, was newly powerful but did not recognize its leadership responsibilities.

Without a hegemon, the world economy collapsed into the great depression. Kindleberger defined the role of the hegemon and explained how it could avert crisis. The hegemon could exercise leadership during a crisis by acting in the following way:

distress	금융
finance	대출
loan	자극하다
stimulate	곤궁에 처해진

demand	동향
counteract	중화하
trend	수요
role	역할

The hegemon would keep its domestic market open, which would allow distressed countries to export. It would provide international finance to countries needing loans and would stimulate demand within its own economy to counteract negative economic trends in other countries. In 1929, though, the U.S. failed to recognize its leadership role and failed to perform any of these roles.

pursue	평가 절하
short term	추구하다
market	시장
devalue	단기

product	악화시키다
implement	위기
exacerbate	시행하다
crisis	제품

- ***Explain hegemonic stability theory***
- ***According to Charles Kindleberger what was the cause of the Great Depression?***

Instead the U.S. pursued its own short term interests. It protected its market from imports.

11.1 Hegemony and Free Trade

Instead of providing a strong dollar for use as an international currency, The U.S. devalued the dollar. The cheap U.S. dollar made foreign products more expensive in the US, preventing other countries from exporting. The U.S. also implemented the protectionist Smoot Hawley Tariff. This U.S. protectionism exacerbated economic crisis in Europe and the US.

long term	장기간	open up	촉진하다
interest	이해	promote	자애로운
react	대응	motivation	동기
create	만들다	benevolent	개방

So the U.S. did not act as a global economic leader. In contrast, a hegemon has enough power to open and organize world markets. Because the hegemon has enough power it can think about its long term interest. The hegemon doesn't merely have to react to the world economy but can use its power to

- ***According to Charles Kindleberger what should a hegemon do during a world economic crisis?***

create rules and institutions to open up the world economy.

11.2 The Hegemon's Free Trade Motives

Why does a hegemon want to promote global economic growth? What is the hegemon's motivation? Liberals and Realists provide two different answers. Liberals believe that the hegemon is benevolent and provides a

public good	공공재	exploitative	상대적인
reward	강압적	relative	착취적인
coercive	보상	self-interest	소득
selfish	이기적인	income	이기적인

public good to other countries. The hegemon gives rewards to other countries and does not use threats or pursue short-term self-interest. Realists, on the other hand, see a coercive hegemon. Realists argue that the hegemon is selfish and exploitative. The hegemon cares only about relative gains. It takes a leadership role for reasons of self-interest. The hegemon likes an open international system because it can gain higher economic growth, more income and greater political power.

force	차단
comply	따르다
cut off	강요하다
share	공동 부담

benefit	위협하다
desire	원하다
stability	안정성
threaten	이득

Realists argue that the hegemon will force other countries to comply. The hegemon can cut off trade, investment and aid. It can force other nations to share the cost of building an open trade system.

How do the two theories explain why states cannot create an open economic system? If all states benefit from an open economic system, why is a leader or hegemon necessary?

11.3 Realist Hegemony Theory

The Realists answer that not all states want a free trade system. Realists argue that the hegemon does want free trade and it has the power to force others to follow the system.

Realists think many other states desire political stability and security. Free trade threatens these other interests.

- ***According to Liberals and Realists, how does the hegemon provide the open trading system?***

competitive	배타적이지 않다
support	지지하다
seek	경쟁력있는
non-exclusive	추구한다

participate	참여한다
principle	통화 제도
non-discrimination	원칙
monetary system	무차별

A hegemon, though, doesn't need to worry political stability or security. The hegemon has the most competitive industry in the world. As the world's dominant power, the hegemon has no real security problems. The hegemon can thus force weaker powers to support free trade.

11.4 Liberal Hegemony Theory

The liberals have a different explanation for why a hegemon is needed for free trade. Liberals believe that all countries seek free trade. Only the hegemon is able to create a free trade system, though. The liberals see an open world trade system as a public good. It is non-exclusive.

Once a free trade system has been created, any country can participate. For example, all countries enjoy the principle

---

- ***According to Realists why does a hegemon want an open world economic system?***
- ***According to Realists why don't non-hegemonic states create an open world economic system?***

of non-discrimination in the World Trade Organization (WTO). All countries enjoy the efficient international monetary system.

exchange rate	무임 승차	manipulate	존재
international currency	소비하다	construct	집단 행동
free rider	환율	collective action	조작하다
consume	국제 통화	existence	만들다

All enjoy the system of stable exchange rates and can use the international currency. Countries will therefore have an incentive to become a free rider. All will want to consume the good, and none will pay the costs. Each state will act to advance its short-term interests. Each will manipulate exchange rates or protect against imports. No state will pay the costs of constructing an open trading system. All will be worse off because of the collective action problem.

The existence of a hegemon can overcome collective action problems, though.

willing to	스스로	incentive	측면
by itself	상관하지 않다	measuring	논란이 많다
contribute	지불	controversial	동기
doesn't care	기꺼이	aspects	측정

A hegemon will provide the public good because it gains

• ***According to Liberals why does a hegemon want an open world economic system?***

so much of the public good by itself. It has an 'encompassing interest.' If the hegemon's economy is large enough, it may receive most of the benefit of a free world trade system. Because the gain is so great, it is willing to pay the costs to build the system by itself. The hegemon's actions are directly related to receiving the gain. It does not need any other nation to contribute. And, the hegemon doesn't care that others will free ride. A similar example might be the case of a rich man who builds a new bridge to his factory in the countryside. He does not care if his poorer neighbors use the bridge as well. His personal gain from building the bridge were greater than his costs, so he built in on his own.

Liberals also argue that a hegemon does not need to force other countries to support free trade. The hegemon can provide positive incentives to support trade. The hegemon only needs to open its market to other countries. This will strengthen exporters in other countries. Those wealthy exporters will then pressure their own governments to favor free trade.

11.5 Measuring Hegemony

Measuring hegemony is one of the controversial aspects of hegemonic stability theory.

unequal	군사의	GNP	접근
military	불평등한	measure	국내총생산
cultural	문화적	range	측정
focus	초점	access	범위

Hegemony requires an extremely unequal division of power. But what type of power and how much power? Is the appropriate type of power military, political, economic, or cultural?

Most scholars focus on shares of world Gross National Product (GNP) or world trade.

But what percentage of GNP is a good measure? If you say 40% of world GNP is required for hegemony, only one country has ever reached that level: the U.S. just after WWII. If you say 20 to 25% of world GNP, America has been stable in that range since the 1930's. But most scholars see a change in the U.S. position over that period. U.C.S.D. Professor David Lake has suggested 15% of world trade as a measure. The problem is that several nations are close to that level today.

There are several other forms of power and other ways to measure hegemony. A broader definition of hegemony would consider access to key raw materials, such as coal and

---

- ***According to Liberals why don't non-hegemonic states create an open world economic system?***
- ***What is an encompassing interest?***

oil, control over capital, and military power to protect the economy. Most measurements of hegemony show a clear decline in U.S. economic power. The U.S. share of world GNP, world manufacturing and world trade has fallen since 1945. There have been at least two periods of hegemony: the period of British hegemony in the 19th century, and the U.S. after World War Two. Portugal, Spain, and the Netherlands have possibly been hegemons as well.

11.6 Hegemonic Stability Theory's View of World History

coal	석탄	industrial	산업
oil	석유	revolution	혁명
decline	쇠퇴	originate	유래되다
coincide	동시에	predominance	우세

There have been two periods in the world economy: in the mid-1800s and the era after 1945. Each of these periods coincided with the rise of either British or American power.

11.61 Great Britain's Hegemony

The United Kingdom used military and economic power to create an open world economy. The industrial revolution originated in the U.K. so British industry quickly achieved global predominance.

output	승리	ideology	예
middle class	중산층	example	사상
triumph	생산량	encourage	장려 하다
elite	엘리트	implement	시행하다

By the mid-1800s, the U.K. accounted for 20% of the world's manufacturing output. The U.K. middle class triumphed, and British elites were committed to an ideology of liberalism. The UK's economic success was an example of the benefits of trade. The U.K.'s example encouraged other states to reduce their tariffs. The U.K. was the first country to implement open trade policies in 1846.

repeal	로비	unprecedented	최고에
Corn Laws	곡물	volume	한번도
grain	곡물조령	repeat	전례 없는
lobby	폐지하다	peak	양

In 1846 the U.K. repealed the Corn Laws, lowering tariffs on imports. The Corn Laws had been used to keep domestic grain prices artificially high. The U.K. and France further increased free trade through the Cobden-Chevalier Trade Treaty. The U.K. opened its domestic markets to products imported from Europe

---

- ***How do scholars usually try to measure hegemony?***
- ***Currently does the world have a strong hegemon according to these measures?***

and North America.

Exporters in Germany and the US, who gained from trade with English, lobbied their home governments for an open trade policy. There was openness in the trade of labor, goods, and capital. Trade within Europe and between Europe and the world grew at unprecedented rates under British hegemony. Capital flowed across borders in volumes that have not been repeated. Millions of people moved from Europe to North America, Latin America, and Australia. British power peaked in the 1870s. Then the power of the U.K. began to decline.

emerge	경쟁자	abandon	흐름
chief	떠올라다	destroy	폐지
rival	빠르게	flow	파괴하다
quickly	최고의	restrict	제한하다

11.62 The Decline of British Hegemony

The U.S. emerged as the U.K.'s chief economic rival by the end of the 1800s. The U.S. rose quickly. In 1820, the U.S. economy was only 33% of the UK. In 1870, the U.K. and U.S. economies were the same size. By World War One the U.S. economy was twice the size of the UK. In the late 1800s, Europe and the U.S. began to abandon free trade.

The world lacked a strong hegemon after World War

• ***Describe the flow of labor, goods, and capital under Great Britain's period of Hegemony.***

One. The war had destroyed the global economy and trade slowed and capital stopped flowing. Governments restricted the movement of people across borders.

unable	자발적으로 나서지 않다	isolation	차별적인
maintain	물러서다	discriminatory	고립
unwilling	유지하다	favor	식민지
retreat	할 수 없는	colony	선호

Great Britain was unable to maintain an open economy, mainly because it lacked sufficient power. The U.S. was sufficiently powerful, but was unwilling to maintain an open economy. It retreated to policies of isolation and protectionism and the world trade system broke apart into discriminatory and protectionist trade groups. The decline in world trade led to the Great Depression in 1929. The U.S. raised its tariffs sharply in 1930. France, Britain and Germany each favored trade with their colonies over foreign countries. Japan did the same in Asia. This system lasted until after World War Two.

- ***How did the U.K. get other countries to open their markets?***
- ***What happened to the world economy during the inter-war period?***
- ***How was the US trade policy during the inter-war period?***

reopen	수용력	competitive.	회복되다
reorganize	재구성	RTAA	호혜통상협정법
capacity	재개하다	GATT	경쟁력
incentive	동기	recover	관세 및 무역에 관한 일반 협정

11.63 U.S. Hegemony

The U.S. became the new hegemon after the war and reopened and reorganized the world economy. After the War, the U.S. produced half of the world's manufactured goods. The U.S. had the capacity and the incentives to create an open world trade system and U.S. industry was finally competitive. Before, U.S. industry could not compete with U.K. products. Now, though, U.S. industry was interested in exports. The U.S. passed the Reciprocal Trade Agreements Act (RTAA) and negotiated 19 treaties lowering tariffs from 1934 to 1938. The U.S. passed GATT, the General Agreement on Tariffs and Trade and created the Marshall Fund to help Western Europe recover.

unilaterally	일방적으로	rely	다자간
institutions	촉진하다	multilateral	유럽 연합
facilitate	관리하다	dominance	지배적인
manage	기관	E.U.	의존하다

Europeans began to import U.S. products. From 1948 to 1958, the U.S. unilaterally lowered its tariff rate, while allowing Europeans to maintain trade protection. By the early 1960s, the European economies had recovered and began to liberalize trade. The new Bretton Woods international institutions then facilitated and managed the newly open economic system.

The U.S. used military, political, economic and ideological power to keep the global system open. The U.S. relied more than the U.K. on institutions and multilateral rules, however, to maintain the system.

11.64 The Decline of U.S. Hegemony

Between 1950 and 1970, the U.S. began to decline. America's global dominance declined. In the 1960s, while Japan's economy grew at 10%, the U.S. economy grew at under 4%. Japan still grew faster than the U.S. in 1970s and 1980s. In the early 1960s, the U.S. produced 40% of the world's products, and Japan produced 5.5% By 1987, though, the U.S. produced 24% and Japan produced 19% Western Europe formed the European Union (E.U).

output	대응
single	산출량
deficits	적자
respond	단일

aggressive	양자간
bilateral	위협하다
threaten	공격적인
deny	거부

The four largest E.U. members (Germany, France, Great Britain, and Italy) produced 22% of world output. The E.U. became the world's largest single market. In the 1980s and 1990s weakening U.S. hegemony was leading to U.S. protectionism. The U.S. ran trade deficits in 1970s,1980s, and

1990s. U.S. competitiveness was declining in high technology industries to Japan and Europe. From 1970 to 1990, while the U.S. share of global high tech markets fell from 30% to 21%, while Japan rose from 7% to 16%.

The U.S. responded with more aggressive trade policy and promoted bilateral trade policies, not multilateral. In the 1980s and 1990s the U.S. pressured Japan to open its market and threatened to deny

access	기록	expense	우세
return	접근	predominance	무임 승차
decline	회귀	free ride	지출
record	쇠퇴	stage	단계

access to U.S. market. Yet even as the U.S. declined, there was not a return to protectionism. Hegemonic stability theory would have predicted a return to protectionism with the decline of the U.S. Some scholars concluded that free trade was possible without hegemon. Other scholars see protectionism under Trump as evidence in favor of hegemonic stability theory.

- ***Which hegemon relied more on multilateral rules and institutions, the US or the UK?***
- ***What happened to the global economic balance of power in the 1980s?***

11.7 Explaining the Hegemon's Decline

11.71 Kennedy's Imperial Overstretch

Hegemonic stability theory explains why a hegemon is needed for free trade, but what can account for the decline of hegemons? Yale historian Paul Kennedy argued that the U.S. hegemon was in decline in the 1980s and the U.S. economy was losing competitiveness. The U.S. government was running budget deficits and accumulating public debt, while the country was also recording large trade deficits. These trends have continued until the present.

Kennedy argued that declining military power follows declining economic power. Kennedy argues that the hegemon must maintain high military expenses to secure military predominance. Other nations don't need to pay as much for defense and they will free ride on the hegemon. Challengers to the hegemon will thus be able to grow their economies faster than the hegemon, eventually becoming more economically powerful than the hegemon. Kennedy believes that hegemons will reach a stage of

---

- ***What type of trade negotiation policy did the US adopt during its period of hegemonic decline?***
- ***Did the US return to protectionism?***

imperial	확대	beyond	능력
overstretch	제국	capacity	국내
expand	제국	challenge	의심하게 합다
empire	확장	domestic	이상으로

imperial overstretch, a condition in which an empire has expanded its territory and military commitments beyond the state's economic capacity. As the hegemon's economic strength declines, the number of security challenges increases, which, in turn, requires even greater military spending. More military spending further weakens the hegemon's economy.

11.72 Olson's Rent Seeking Groups

Other scholars, such as Mancur Olson, provide domestic explanations for hegemonic decline.

rent	추구하는	non-productive	로비
seeking	낭비	private gain	유리한
phenomenon	현상	lobby	비생산적인
waste	지대	favorable	자신의 이익

Olson argues that 'rent seeking' groups play an important

- ***What is Paul Kennedy's explanation for US hegemonic decline?***
- ***According to Kennedy, what should a hegemon do to stop declining?***

role in hegemonic decline. Rent seeking is a phenomenon where economic actors waste economic resources through non-productive activities to pursue private gain, such as through lobbying, or taking others wealth. Rent seeking groups organize to lobby for favorable government policies.

protection	허가	special	돌아가다
subsidies	세금	benefit	특별한
license	보호	interfere	방해하다
tax	보조금	pass on	이득

These types of government policies include trade protection, government subsidies, government licenses, or tax benefits. These groups try to gain a special, private benefit from the government. This special benefit is called a 'rent,' which can be calculated through the sale of products at above the market rate or purchase of products at below the market price.

Rent seeking groups also want to protect their wealth by limiting competition. Limited competition interferes with the market and makes the economy less efficient. These costs are passed on to the general public.

general public	자원	accumulate	사회적인
resource	경향이 있다	eliminated	제거
piece of pie	대중	societal	더 많이 느는
tend	파이 조각	revolution	혁명

- ***What is a rent seeking group?***

Each of these rent seeking groups also wastes resources by lobbying the government. The groups spend their resources on politics, not on economic production. Proliferation of rent seeking groups leads to a decrease in the economic growth rate. Each of these groups is trying to increase their individual piece of the pie rather than to grow the whole pie. Olsen argued that stable societies with unchanged political institutions tend to accumulate more of these groups over time. It takes a considerable amount of time for a nation to become a hegemon, during which the number of rent seeking groups can grow. These groups can only be eliminated through a major war or societal revolution.

argue	주장	consume	소모하다
absence	부재	otherwise	달리
eliminate	지주	industrialization	비난을 받다
land-lord	제거하다	blame	산업화

Olson argues that the number of rent seeking groups has grown in England and the U.S., and that the absence of rent seeking groups explains the high rate of economic growth in Germany and Japan after World War Two. The theory could also be applied to explain Korean economic growth

---

- ***What is a rent seeking group?***
- ***According to Mancur Olson, how does rent-seeking lead to hegemonic decline?***

after the Korean War, which helped to eliminate the powerful rent seeking landlord class. Landlords had been consuming resources that could otherwise be used for industrialization. Powerful landlord groups have been blamed for slowing economic development in Latin America and Africa.

decades	로비스트	permanent	개업
lobbyist	관리	attorney	변호사
management	수십 년	practicing law	상설
association	협회	finance	금융

Lobbying activity certainly does seem to have increased in the U.S. in recent decades. The evidence includes the number of companies with lobbyists in Washington D.C. Companies spent $3.5 billion in 2010 to lobby the U.S. federal government, compared to $1.4 billion in 1998. The number of management associations and labor unions with permanent offices in Washington DC has increased. Also the number of attorneys in Washington D.C. not practicing law has increased. They are all involved in lobbying. Major lobbying industries include health, finance,

insurance	비용을 전가 시키다	general public	의료 산업
communications	통신	health care industry	결탁
membership	회원국	qualifications	자격
shifting cost	보험	collude	대중

- ***How does Olson explain the rise of Japan and Germany after WW II?***

insurance and communications. American rent seeking groups are very good at increasing the income of their membership and shifting costs onto the general public. One example is in the American health care industry. American doctors have increased their salaries by raising the qualifications and costs needed to become a doctor. Hospitals and insurance companies have also colluded

pass on	법적 비용	lawyers	잘 조직된
health care	비교하여	well organized	정치적으로 영향력있는
in comparison	의료	politically influential	변호사
legal expense	부과하다	per capita	일인당

to pass high costs on to patients. The U.S. now has one of the most expensive health care systems in the world. Americans paid an average of $7,538 a year in medical costs in 2008. In comparison, in Great Britain, Norway and Switzerland the average was $2,995. The U.S. spent three times more on health care in 2008 than in 1990. Americans also spend great amounts on legal expenses. American lawyers are a very well organized, politically influential group. The United States also has the most lawyers per capita in the OECD and the world.

- ***Is there evidence to support Olson's idea?***
- ***How is rent seeking related to expensive U.S. health care?***

OECD	보유고	liquid	사용되다
currency	통화	transaction	교량
international	경제 협력 개발 기구	in circulation	유동성 있는
reserves	외환	bridge	거래

11.73 Hegemony and Currency Overvaluation

There are also international economic explanations for a hegemon's economic decline. As the center of world's economy, the hegemon's currency will become the world's currency. This is true of the U.S. dollar. The U.S. dollar is used as international reserves by many countries, as the most liquid currency in the world, used in 85% of all international currency transactions. Most of the U.S. dollars in circulation are also used outside of the U.S. The U.S. dollar is commonly used as a bridge between two other currencies, and thus is referred to as a 'bridge currency.'

bank	은행	international reserve	중심
exchange	외국인	core	핵심
foreigners	교환	trusted	외환보유고
hold	보유	center	신뢰받는

So, if a bank wants to exchange Korean Won into Thai Baht, the Korean currency is first changed into U.S. dollars and then changed from U.S. dollars into Thai currency. This is because there is always sufficient supply and demand for U.S. dollars in every country, so the exchange costs are very low.

The supply and demand for Thai Baht, on the other hand, is not very high in Korea. Why do foreigners hold so many dollars as international reserve? The U.S. economy and the U.S. government are at the core of the world's economy. The U.S. currency is therefore the most trusted of all currencies. The 2008 financial crisis demonstrated the high level of international trust in the U.S. government and U.S. economy. Even though the world financial crisis was centered in the US,

value	과대평가되다
crisis	위기
public debt	가치
overvalue	국가채무

uncompetitive	사라지다
industrial base	산업 기반
disappear	경쟁력 없는
capital	자본

the value of the U.S. dollar rose during the financial crisis. Foreigners increased purchases of U.S. government debt in the midst of the U.S. financial crisis. Foreigners considered U.S. government debt as an extremely safe investment during unstable times. The world, therefore, has a high demand for the hegemon's currency and a high demand for the hegemon government's public debt. The result of this high demand is that the hegemon's currency will become overvalued and expensive and the hegemon's government will increase its

---

- ***Why do foreigners want to hold dollars?***
- ***How does the international importance of the U.S. dollar weaken the U.S. economy?***

debt. An overvalued currency will make the hegemon's exports expensive and uncompetitive overseas. The hegemon's industrial base will weaken as a result. In fact, America's basic manufacturing industry has largely disappeared during the last fifty years. Increased debt means the hegemon is consuming more now, but less in the future. Increased government debt means less capital for private investment.

ultimately	증거	defense spending	참여했다
weaken	차지하고	been involved	명확한
evidence	궁극적으로	simultaneous	국방지출
accounts for	약화시키다	clear	동시에

Debt makes it harder to grow the economy in the future and further decreases the hegemon's economic power. So, it may be that being the center of the world economy ultimately weakens the hegemon's economy.

11.8 Is the U.S. in Decline?

What does the evidence show? Has the U.S. hegemon declined or not? The U.S. accounts for half of all world defense spending and has recently been involved in two simultaneous wars in Iraq and Afghanistan. High U.S. defense spending would appear to harm the U.S. economy. U.S. defense spending has declined as a percentage of government spending, though, and as percentage of GDP since the 1950s.

It is also not clear that military spending is always harmful to economic growth.

research	혁신	critic	일정한
development	연구	constant	비평가
innovation	개발	productivity	중
information technology	정보 기술	among	생산력

Military research and development need not always hurt the economy. Innovations in transportation, communications and information technology was the result of military research and development in World War One and World War Two.

Critics of U.S. decline also show that the U.S. share of the world economy has remained constant at 25% from the 1970s and has not decline. U.S. productivity is also among the highest in the world.

lead	매력적인	education	사회적 통합
key	인구	resources	교육
attractive	앞장서가다	social unity	자원
population	주요	alliances	동맹

The U.S. continues to lead in key high-technology

- ***Is the U.S. hegemon declining? What does the evidence show?***
- ***What are the pro and con arguments?***
- ***What is 'soft power'?***

industries. The U.S. is also very attractive to foreign investors. The U.S. continues to have many sources of power: population, education, resources, social unity, political stability, military power, alliances, and ideological appeal.

ideological	자본가	mass-consumption	대중소비
appeal	이의를 제기 하다	magazine	습관
democratic	이념적	tastes	잡지
capitalist	민주주의의	habit	취향

Joseph Nye claimed that many scholars ignore the importance of U.S. "soft power." The U.S. is popular due to its democratic, capitalist, and mass-consumption culture. U.S. television, movies and magazines affect global cultural tastes and habits. Nye argues that America's positive popular image keeps other nations from opposing U.S. power.

budget	감세	generate	침체
tax cuts	유입	instability	만들다
interest rate	이자율	recession	개방
inflow	예산	openness	불안정

11.81 A Decline in Threats after the Cold War

Critics also point out that the U.S. budget and trade deficits are the result of policies, which can be changed. Deficits resulted from tax cuts in the early 1980s, which increased budget deficits and raised interest rates. This increased capital inflows and helped generate the trade deficits. Recently global instability and economic recession have led to capital inflows, trade deficits and budget deficits.

The U.S. decline in power has not lead to the end of openness (until Trump, that is).

international institutions		완결하다		round		세계 무역 기구
kept open		에도 불구하다		bargaining		라운드
despite		국제 기관		WTO		흥정
complete		개방 유지시키다		intellectual property		지적 재산권

Liberals claim that international institutions have kept the world economy open despite the U.S. decline. Governments have strengthened the multilateral trade system. States completed three rounds of trade bargaining since 1970, which further reduced tariffs. Governments also established the World Trade Organization (WTO) and created multilateral rules for intellectual property and trade in services.

persist		사회적인		repeal		곡물조령
domestic		기관적		Corn Laws		확실하게
societal		지속		definitively		폐지
institutional		국내		prediction		예측

Liberals believe that international institutions and free trade can persist without a hegemon. We will find out.

- ***What is the liberal explanation for continued openness after the hegemon's decline?***

Chapter

12 Testing the Different Trade Theories

The book has examined a variety of different explanations for trade policy, including domestic, societal theories like the factors model and sectors model, political institutional approaches and two different versions of hegemonic stability theory. This chapter will test these different theories to see which one can best explain the case of the repeal of the Corn Laws in England. More cases are needed to definitively test these different theories, but this exercise shows how to utilize a theory to make predictions about trade policy and how to apply a theory to a case.

apply	곡물	repeal	폐지
case	자극하다	hegemon	개인적인 이득
stimulate	케이스	motivated	패권국
grain	적용합니다	private gain	동기

12.1 The Corn Laws

What were the Corn Laws? During the Napoleonic wars in Europe, Britain established the Corn Laws to stimulate domestic grain production. The laws were a form of protection which only permitted imports if the price of grain rose above a certain price. Britain adopted free trade when it repealed the Corn Laws on June 26, 1846, marking the first time a powerful economic state adopted free trade. How well do each of the theories explain Britain's policy change?

Liberal Hegemonic Stability Theory assumes that the hegemon is motivated by private gain to pay for an open world trading system. The hegemon provides an open world trading system because the private gain from creating the system is greater than the hegemon's private costs.

account	차지하다	capability	문제가 있는
GDP	국내총생산	timing	타이밍
competitive	경쟁력있는	problematic	우위에 서다
industrialized	산업화된	achieve	능력

For this to be true, though, the hegemon's GDP must account for a very large percentage of the world GDP. British GDP in

---

- ***What were the Corn Laws?***
- ***What is a weakness in the Liberal Hegemonic Stability explanation for the repeal of the Corn Laws?***

1846 was not the largest in the world, however. In fact Britain's GDP was less than half the size of Chinese GDP, and Britain's economy was also smaller than the Indian economy. Even within Europe, British GDP was smaller than Russian GDP in 1850 and about equal to that of Germany and France. Britain may not have received a large enough private gain to pay the costs of building and maintaining the world trading system. Realist hegemonic stability theory would predict Britain would liberalize international trade in pursuit of greater political power. In 1850, as the world's first industrialized nation Britain had the world's most competitive industries and would therefore desire an open trading structure. Britain had the interest and capability to control the international political economy.

But, problems undermine with the Realist view. First, the timing is problematic. The Realist version of hegemonic stability theory would expect Britain to immediately use military might to force other nations to follow the rules of its free trade system. Yet while Britain achieved military dominance in 1815, it did not promote free-trade until the 1840s.

weaken	약화시키다	factors	기계
naval	위상	interest rate	요소
dominance	일방적	machinery	보험
unilateral	해군	insurance	이자율

Also, Britain's military power was weakening. Britain's naval dominance had declined from 1815 to 1846. So the timing of free trade did not coincide with Britain's peak in military strength. Also, Britain had unilaterally liberalized trade, in contrast to Realist expectations that a hegemon would use its power to open up other country's markets. But Britain had not used force to open up trade with other European powers. Britain had liberalized free trade without asking other nations to do so in return.

The factors model, a domestic political explanation, can provide some insight. Capital and labor were abundant factors in Britain. As the first industrialized country, Britain had the most capital per worker in the world. Britain's capital abundance can also be measured by its interest rate, which was the world's lowest. Britain used the most machinery in the world and enjoyed the world's highest level of technology. British banking and insurance industries dominated world financial markets and were quite profitable.

repeal	폐지	output	생산물
manufactured goods	귀족	maintain	되는건
agricultural	농업	obtain	유지하다
aristocrats	제조품	equal	얻다

British cities like London were the largest in the world, abundant in labor. According to the factors model, workers

---

• ***What is a weakness in the Realist Hegemonic Stability explanation for the repeal of the Corn Laws?***

and capitalists should have preferred free trade. Capitalists did support the repeal of the Corn Laws. Free trade would also lower grain prices and food prices, allowing capitalists to reduce the wages they paid to labor. Free trade would also allow capitalists to increase profits by exporting more manufactured goods.

British labor also wanted to repeal the Corn Laws. Lower grain prices from free trade allowed workers to spend less on food, providing workers more money to spend on other goods. As predicted by the factors model, the British agricultural aristocrats opposed repealing the Corn Laws. The Corn Laws had raised the price of their output, and maintained their incomes. The factors model succeeds in predicting the interests of Britain's major economic groups. Groups also need economic power to obtain political power. Capitalists and workers were also economically powerful.

But economic power does not automatically equal political power.

collective action	개혁	House of Lords	입법
overcome	집단 행동	legislative	의회
reform	극복하다	assembly	상원
advantage	이점	House of Commons	하원

Political power requires political action. How easily can each group organize its members to take political action? Can the group overcome the collective action problem? Political institutions can affect how easily groups overcome collective action problems, which leads to the conclusion that we should examine British political institutions. In fact, reforms had weakened the Aristocrats institutional advantage. Only aristocrats were represented in the British House of Lords, a powerful legislative assembly. Aristocrats had used their power in the House of Lords to influence voting in the House of Commons to maintain the Corn Laws.

parliament	설명	GATT	원칙
representation	이동	WTO	세계 무역 기구
Shift	대표	principle	수립
explanation	의회	form	관세 및 무역에 관한 일반 협정

Institutional reform made repeal of the Corn Laws possible. The Reform Act of 1832 reduced the power of aristocrats in parliament giving representation in the House of Commons to newly formed large cities and increasing the number of voters able to vote to 17% of the population.

This institutional reform shifted power to new industrial capitalists. The institutional factor is thus an important part of a domestic political explanation for British support for free trade

---

- ***What is the Domestic Factors Model analysis of the repeal of the Corn Laws?***
- ***What is a weakness in the Domestic Factors Model explanation for the repeal of the Corn Laws?***

policies in 1846. So, while international factors provided Britain with an interest in pursuing free trade, they do not explain the timing or process by which Britain revoked the Corn Laws. Domestic factors, particularly the power and interests of economic classes as predicted by the factors model and the nature of British political institutions best explain the timing of Britain's adoption of a free trade policy.

- ***How were institutions important in the repeal of the Corn Laws?***

Part IV

The Modern Trade System and Rise of Regionalism

This final chapter examines the development of the modern trading system. The modern trade system is organized around the General Agreement on Tariffs and Trade (GATT) and the World Trade Organization (WTO). This chapter examines why the GATT and WTO were formed and examines how these institutions function and the key principles on which they were formed.

characterize	일방적	manage	관리하다
unilateral	밀다	victorious	확실히
bilateral	양자간	ensure	보호주의
push	특징있다	protectionism	승전국

Chapter

13 G.A.T.T.

The modern trade system begins with the story of the GATT. Before the Second World War, the international trade system was characterized by mostly unilateral action and bilateral treaties. This changed after the war with a push for international institutions to help manage the system. After the war, the two main victorious powers, the U.S. and the U.K., wanted to ensure that protectionism and

Great Depression	마련	employment	기초
lay	토대	basis	고용
groundwork	대공황	multilateral	국제 무역 기구
postwar	전후	ITO	다자간

the Great Depression would not be repeated. Discussions between the U.S. and U.K. in 1943 laid the groundwork for postwar trade negotiations. A U.S. State Department document on trade and employment formed the basis for multilateral negotiations that resulted in the Havana Charter, which was also known as the Charter for the International Trade Organization or the ITO.

full-fledged	자격을 제대로 갖춘	ratify	구상하다
organization	상업의	drafted	보호 주의자
deal with	조직	protectionist	비준하다
commercial	다루다	fear	두려움은

The ITO was to be a full-fledged organization, which would deal with development, employment, investment, and commercial policy and be part of the UN system. But the ITO was never created because the U.S. Congress didn't ratify the Havana Charter, even though U.S. President, Harry Truman, had drafted the ITO proposal. Powerful U.S. protectionists feared that the ITO

sovereignty	자유무역 지지자	submit	비공식
free trader	예외	charter	자동적으로
exception	약관	by default	헌장
clause	주권	informal	제출하다

would increase competition and reduce U.S. sovereignty. Free traders in the U.S. also opposed the ITO's numerous

---

- ***What type of treaty was common in the international trade system before WW II?***

exception clauses. Wary of defeat, President Truman refused to submit the ITO charter to the U.S. Congress to be ratified, and so the U.S. failed to approve of the ITO. During bargaining over the ITO, 23 governments began negotiations, and ratified the GATT in October 1947 as part of the ITO. When the ITO charter failed to gain U.S. support, the GATT became an institution by default. The resulting GATT was only a trade agreement, however rather than a treaty. As a trade agreement, GATT did not require ratification by the U.S. Congress. The GATT was informal,

limited	주로	code	회원국
legal	법적	behavior	행동
obligations	제한된	non-tariff barriers	규칙
primarily	책임이	membership	비관세 장벽

with limited legal obligations and was primarily a written code of behavior on international trade. The GATT helped to reduce tariffs, then reduced the use of Non-Tariff Barriers, while increasing its membership.

flexibility	협력하다	recovery	동맹
circumstance	냉전	alliance	회복
Cold War	유연성이	accepted	목적
cooperate	환경	objectives	받아 들다

- ***What was the ITO?***
- ***Why wasn't the ITO implemented?***

GATT succeeded in reducing tariffs from an average of 40% in 1947 to 4% in 2000. Why was GATT so successful? Some liberal scholars claimed that GATT's flexibility allowed it to be more effective and able to adapt to changing circumstances. Realists provided different reasons for GATTs effectiveness in the 1950s and 1960s in promoting economic liberalization and growth. Realists argued that the Cold War raised the US's incentives to cooperate economically with Western Europe and Japan. By promoting economic recovery within its partners, the U.S. could increase the strength of the anti-Soviet alliance. As the global hegemon, the U.S. was able and willing to provide leadership. There were a relatively small number of major allies, which were all industrialized democracies,so they accepted U.S. leadership. The GATT promoted free trade, but also allowed member governments to pursue domestic policy objectives like full employment.

full employment	접근
basic	다자간
approach	기본
multilateral	완전 고용

issue	문제
compromise	안전 장치
safeguards	추구하다
pursue	타협

- ***What was GATT? How was it different from the ITO?***
- ***What is the Liberal explanation for GATT success?***
- ***What is the Realist explanation for GATT success?***

13.1 The GATT Principle of Liberalization

GATT's principles and ruleswere not totally new. GATT's basic approach called for trade policy through negotiation, a method which had been established through the U.S.'s Reciprocal Trade Agreements Act. GATT, though, relied on multilateral negotiations, which take place when many countries come together to negotiate over one issue. GATT reflected a political compromise. While GATT liberalized trade, GATT also included safeguards to allow member nations to pursue

social	국제수지	remove	할당량
stable	안정적인	barriers	제거한다
balance of payments	사회적인	control	제어
liberalize	자유화하다	quota	장벽

domestic social policies and maintain a stable balance of payments. GATT had four key principles. The first principle was liberalizing trade. All GATT members agreed on the goal to gradually remove barriers to trade. GATT first liberalized trade by lowering tariffs, and then by controlling the use of Non-Tariff Barriers (NTB)s like quotas.

- ***What was GATT's basic approach to negotiations?***
- ***How was GATT a compromise?***

production	제거
block	확장
expansion	저지
elimination	생산

round	처리
address	라운드
hold	개최
initially	처음에

GATT preferred that countries use tariffs and not quotas. Tariffs allowed exporters to increase production. Quotas, on the other hand, set a limit, blocking expansion of trade. So, GATT's Article 11 called for the elimination of quotas.

GATT liberalized trade through a series of 'rounds' of negotiations. Here is a list of the major GATT rounds, including the main issues each negotiation addressed and the number of participating countries.

GATT Trade Rounds

Name	Start	Duration	Countries	Subjects
Geneva	1947	7 months	23	Tariffs
Annecy	1949	5 months	34	Tariffs
Torquay	1950	8 months	34	Tariffs
Geneva II	1956	5 months	22	Tariffs, admission of Japan
Dillon	1960	11 months	45	Tariffs
Kennedy	1964	37 months	48	Tariffs, anti-dumping
Tokyo	1973	74 months	102	Tariffs, non-tariff measures, "framework" agreements

Uruguay	1986	87 months	123	Tariffs, non-tariff measures, rules, services, intellectual property, dispute settlement, textiles, agriculture, creation of WTO, etc.

The first round of negotiations between 23 nations was held in 1947 and took a few months. Initially negotiations were held over tariffs on individual products.

complicate	무조건	health care	관세 동맹
entire	최혜국	restaurants	예외
significantly	국산품과 같은 처리	nondiscrimination	호혜통상협정법
service industry	제품	dimensions	자동적으로

Negotiation in trade rounds became more complicated as more members joined GATT. So, from the Kennedy Round, negotiations were held to lower tariffs of a range of products in entire industries. By the last GATT round, the Uruguay Round, 123 nations negotiated over 7 years. GATT significantly liberalized tariffs but did not address certain parts of the economy. GATT never addressed agricultural products, or the service industry, which includes a range of industries such as health care, insurance, hotels and restaurants.

• ***How did GATT liberalize trade?***

13.2 The GATT Principle of Non-Discrimination

The second major GATT principle was nondiscrimination. There were two dimensions

products	무조건	automatically	호혜통상협정법
MFN	국산품과 같은 처리	exception	자동적으로
National Treatment	최혜국	RTA	예외
unconditionally	제품	customs union	관세 동맹

of nondiscrimination: nondiscrimination towards products outside of the nation which was also known as External Non-discrimination, or Most Favored Nation (MFN) treatment, and nondiscrimination towards foreign goods once they enter another's nation domestic economy, which was known as Internal Non-discrimination, or National Treatment. The MFN clause was contained in GATT's Article 1. According to MFN, every trade advantage given to one other country must be unconditionally and automatically extended to all GATT member nations. So, for example, if Germany and France agree to lower tariffs on each other's auto imports, they must also lower tariffs on autos imported from other GATT members.

GATT contained some exceptions to MFN, however. GATT

- ***How were early rounds different from later rounds?***
- ***What were the two dimensions of non-discrimination?***
- ***What was MFN status?***

allowed for the formation of regional trade groups. Members of a Regional Trade Agreement, or RTA could provide one another with special benefits and would not be required to extend tariff cuts to other non-RTA member nations that were GAT members. RTAs took the form of free trade areas and customs union, such as N.A.F.T.A. and the E.U.

preferential	연방	discriminate	동일한
former	특혜의	taxation	차별하다
colonies	식민지	regulations	과세
Commonwealth	전	identical	규칙

GATT also allowed developing nations to receive preferential treatment. One such example would be the case of advanced nations providing trade benefits to former colonies, such as the British providing low tariffs to members of the British Commonwealth.

In addition to MFN, GATT also contained the principle of National Treatment. GATT member nations could not discriminate domestically against foreign products. This means that after a foreign product has been imported, the foreign product must be treated similarly to domestic products. Taxation and regulations must be identical. So, for example, Australian beef sold at Home Plus cannot be taxed at a higher

---

- ***Were there exceptions to MFN status? What were they?***
- ***What was National Treatment?***

rate than Korean beef.

reciprocity	유혹	free ride	논리
concessions	양보	logic	그 대가로
basis	상호주의	pressure	무임 승차
tempting	기초	in return	압력

13.3 The GATT Principle of Reciprocity

GATT's third principle was reciprocity. To receive you must also give. Trade concessions were to be negotiated on reciprocal basis. The principle of reciprocity was to limit free riding under the most favored nation principle. One can imagine how tempting it would be for nations to free ride on MFN, since they could receive the benefits of other nation's concessions, without giving any concessions. The reciprocity principle gave nations an incentive to open their markets. There was a political logic to the reciprocity principle, too. Companies wanting to export would pressure their home governments to open the domestic markets, if these companies expected foreign nations to open their markets in return.

volume	선수를 치다	exclude	접근
offer	제공	talks	제외하다
initiative	량	genuine	진짜의
LDC	최빈개도국	access	협상

The reciprocity principle was also preferred by the major trading states. These economically powerful nations had the largest markets and highest trade volume. They could offer the most to other nations, which also provided them with the most power. Usually the most powerful nations dominated GATT negotiations. The U.S., E.U., and Japan normally took the initiative. Usually LDCs were excluded from talks until the very end. In 1982, four groups of nations established 'the Quad,' comprised of the EU, U.S., Japan and Canada, to lead trade discussions. The U.S. accused Japan of not providing genuine reciprocal access to its markets,

share	불공정한	exception	영향
comparative advantage	비교 우위	temporary	일반적인 제외 조항
unfair	몫	GEC	예외
safeguards	안전 장치	ramifications	일시적인

and demanded access to a certain share of the Japanese market. Japan responded that it had a comparative advantage over the U.S., not unfair trade advantages.

- ***How did the principle of reciprocity work?***
- ***Which domestic groups were empowered by the principle of reciprocity?***
- ***Which countries favored the reciprocity principle?***

13.4 The GATT Principle of Safeguards

GATT's fourth principle was that of safeguards. There were safeguards to protect member nations from the negative effects of free trade. There were two sets of circumstances in which exceptions to free trade were allowed. Usually these exceptions were temporary. The first type of exception was known as the General Escape Clause (GEC). A country could demand a GEC, when domestic conditions were difficult and the threat of free trade to an industry would have major ramifications.

enacted	도덕	ISI	수입대체 산업화
morality	일시적으로	dumping	보조금을 주다
national security	제정	levy	덤핑
temporarily	국가 안보	subsidize	부과

Permanent safeguards could be enacted to protect public morality and health, preserve natural resources, and uphold national security. Import restrictions were also temporarily allowed to enable Import Substitution Industrialization (ISI) policies and in times of balance of payment troubles.

Safeguards could also be used in cases where other nations used unfair trade practices, such as by dumping. Dumping

---

- ***Who were the Quad?***
- ***Why did GATT have safeguards?***
- ***What was a GEC?***

occurs when a firm sells products overseas at a lower price than in its domestic market, or at a price lower than the cost of production. GATT allowed countries to levy anti-dumping customs taxes in these situations. GATT also allowed countries to levy customs taxes against countries that subsidized their exports.

countervailing	지속성 있는	NICS	신흥 공업국가
duties	관세	consistent	대응
exemptions	상계	respond	일치하는
persistent	면제	textile	직물

These customs taxes were called Countervailing Duties (CVD), used against countries that subsidize exports by providing low interest government loans or tax exemptions. The U.S. was the first and largest user of CVDs. U.S. imposed 58% of all CVDs from 1980 to 1992, because of persistent U.S. balance of trade deficits.

- ***When could permanent safeguards be used?***
- ***What is dumping?***

13.5 The Era of New Protectionism

After two decades of tariff reduction under GATT, the world trading system entered a period of "New Protectionism" in the 1970s and 1980s. There were major changes in the world economic system during this period. Industries in Japan and the NICS began to compete with those in the U.S. and Europe in the 1970s. Beginning in 1971, the U.S. began to suffer from consistent trade deficits. The U.S. responded with protection in textiles,

footwear	반도체	barrier	입장
VRA	자율 규제 계약	aggressive	일방적
semiconductor	가격 차이	unilateral	공격적인
price difference	신발	stance	장벽

footwear, steel, and automobiles. The New Protection came in the form of Non-Tariff Barriers (NTB)s: especially Voluntary Restraints Agreements (VRAs).

The U.S. forced its trading partners to adopt VRAs in the late 1980 in the semiconductor and auto industries. Foreign producers agreed to limit exports to the U.S. because it was better than tariffs. Why? Faced with the likelihood that their exports would cost more, U.S. trade partners sought to avoid tariffs, where the price difference would go to the

---

- ***What is a CVD? Who used them most?***
- ***What led to the period of 'New Protectionism'?***

U.S. government as a tax. With a VRA, producers could keep the higher price. VRAs acted as a barrier to trade in the steel, clothing, textiles, footwear, and automobile industries. European nations increasingly relied on subsidies for protection. Instead of blocking lower price imports, these nations lowered the costs of their domestic producers through subsidies.

GATT had difficulty controlling NTBs, which proved to be very difficult to measure. By 2000, NTBs affected about 17.5% of goods imported into industrialized nations and 60% of developing nation imports. The growth in NTBs led the U.S. to shift to a more aggressive, unilateral stance on trade.

unfair	무역 대표부	begun	시작
practices	겨냥	emerge	할당량
USTR	관행	ignore	출현
target	불공정한	quotas	무시하다

The U.S. began to use Section 301 of the 1974 trade laws on unfair practices to tax imports. The U.S. Congress instructed the U.S. Trade Representative to identify nations using unfair practices and threaten them with sanctions The USTR targeted Japan, India, and Brazil in the early 1990s. By the late 1990s several problems with GATT had begun to emerge.

- ***How did American protectionism differ from European protectionism?***
- ***How did the US use Section 301?***

GATT had ignored many important trade issues. For instance, GATT hadn't addressed protectionism in agriculture and textiles. In fact, GATT had allowed export subsidies and import quotas in agriculture and textiles,

restraint	협정	formal	피하다
multi-fiber	클럽	waive	공식적인
arrangement	섬유	violation	위반
club	규제	circumvent	보류

such as bilateral export restraints in the 1950s and the multilateral multi-fiber arrangement. GATT had also never enforced any sanctions against members. GATT members were more of a club than a formal organization. Members could easily waive regulations, and ignore violations. Countries could also circumvent GATT's

dispute	처리	resolve	충돌
settlement	절차	conflict	위반하다
procedure	부적당	fairly	공정하다
inadequate	분쟁	violate	해결하다

ban on import quotas by imposing VERs. GATT's weak dispute settlement procedures were also inadequate to resolve conflicts fairly. GATT's principles were often violated. For

---

- ***Which trade issues did GATT ignore?***
- ***How strong were GATT's rules and principles?***

instance the nondiscrimination principle was threatened by Regional Trade Agreements that didn't follow MFN treatment.

balance of trade	적자	specific	상호주의
deficit	강화	reciprocity	소홀했던
enhance	비교 우위	range	특정한
comparative advantage	무역 수지	neglected	범위

To address these shortcomings, the U.S. began to seek changes with GATT. With a growing balance of trade deficit, the U.S. charged other nations with unfair trading. The U.S. wanted to enhance GATT's authority, especially in the areas of services, intellectual property, agriculture and investment, which were all areas in which the U.S. enjoyed comparative advantage. The U.S. also wanted to gain specific reciprocity from its trading partners. These issues were taken up in Uruguay Round negotiations, which began in 1986 and continued until 1993. The Uruguay Round attempted to deal with wide range of neglected issues, including intellectual property, investment, services, and agriculture.

propose	제안하다	reservation	임시로
European Community	지지하다	sovereignty	즉석
support	제안	ad hoc	주권
proposal	유럽 공동체	provisionary	의구심

- ***Why did the US want to reform GATT?***
- ***What did the Uruguay Round try to address?***

Chapter

14 The W.T.O.

14.1 The Establishment of the WTO

Up to 123 nations participated in the Uruguay Round, which led to longer, more complicated negotiations. In April 1990, Canada proposed creating a World Trade Organization to replace the GATT. The European Community also supported the proposal, but the U.S. had reservations, fearing a loss of sovereignty. The different countries reached a compromise, though, and the WTO replaced the GATT in January 1995.

There were several differences between the WTO and GATT. The GATT was ad hoc and provisionary, mainly because the General Agreement had never been ratified in member

---

• ***Which countries supported the WTO proposal?***

ratify	비준하다		constituted	복귀
parliament	영구적인		revert	상태
provision	항목		status	확고
permanent	의회		sound	구성된

country parliaments. GATT contained no provisions for the creation of an official organization. The WTO and its agreements, on the other hand, were permanent. The WTO is a formal, legally constituted organization like the IMF and the World Bank. Under the WTO, the GATT didn't disappear, but it reverted to its original status as an agreement for trade in goods. As an international organization, the WTO has a sound

basis	자체		cover	일치
themselves	근거		binding	구속력
function	처리		consensus	적용
deal with	기능		block	막다

legal basis. WTO members ratified the WTO agreements, and the agreements themselves describe how the WTO is to function.

- ***In terms of organizational structure, how was the WTO different than GATT?***
- ***After the WTO was formed what happened to GATT?***
- ***How were disputes settled in the WTO compared to the GATT?***

The GATT dealt with trade in goods. The WTO, though, covers services and intellectual property as well. The WTO dispute settlement system is also faster, and more binding than the old GATT system. WTO rulings cannot be blocked by one member, as under GATT. In fact, a consensus of member states is required to block WTO panel reports.

appeal	패널	implement	권고
appellate	기구	recommendation	거부
body	상소	refuse	시행하다
panel	이의를 제기	complainant	제기하는 국가

A WTO member can appeal a dispute settlement decision to the appellate body. If the appellate body agrees with the panel report, the member must implement the panel's recommendations. If a country still refuses to follow the WTO report, the complainant nation

authorize	권한이 있다	swift	납득시키다
retaliate	운영	justice	정의
operate	전망	convince	신속한
prospect	보복하다	engaging in	에 참여

are authorized to retaliate. The WTO operates according to the one nation one vote principle, like GATT. LDCs didn't have

- ***Which countries set the WTO agenda?***
- ***Which institution was busier with complaints? WTO or GATT?***

as much influence as expected, though, in the WTO. Instead, the OECD and Group of Seven play a major role in setting the WTO's agenda. The prospects of swifter justice convinced governments to bring their trade disputes to the WTO, instead of engaging in

retaliation	보복	structure	유지하다
complaint	생산	maintain	확신
output	불만	investor	투자자
principles	원칙	confidence	구조

retaliation. So, in three years, the WTO dealt with 132 complaints. By comparison, in 47 years, GATT heard only 300 complaints. World trade also increased rapidly under the WTO. Trade grew at 9.5%, three times faster than global economic output.

14.2 Comparing WTO and GATT

The WTO and GATT can be compared according to their principles, structure, dispute settlement system and central issues. The WTO maintained the GATT principle of non-discrimination. Each nation received MFN status and its products received national treatment. The WTO also maintained the GATT principle of trade liberalization through negotiation. The WTO wanted to provide foreign companies, investors and governments with confidence that trade barriers would not be raised

arbitrarily	관행	flexibility	운영
address	예외	privileges	이득
exceptions	독단적으로 구축	adjust	융통성
discourage	처리	run	적응

arbitrarily. The WTO also addressed some of the exceptions of GATT. The WTO discouraged unfair export subsidies and the practice of dumping. The WTO also provided more benefits to LDCs, by giving them flexibility, special privileges, and time to adjust to open trade.

The WTO is run by its member governments. Unlike the GATT, the WTO has

permanent	일치	Ministerial	회의
consensus	위원회	conference	문제
council	영구적인	matter	각료회의
committee	회의	handle	처리

permanent decision making bodies. All major WTO decisions are made by the membership as a whole. Decisions are taken by consensus, through various councils and committees. The WTO's top organization is the Ministerial Conference, with the authority to take decisions on all matters. It meets at least once every two years. The WTO's everyday

---

• ***What were the WTO promise to LDCs?***

work is handled by three other bodies.

composed of	판결하다	TPRB	무역정책검토기구
oversee	구성	ensure	집행
panels	감독하다	notify	보장
adjudicate	패널	enforce	알려 드리다

The WTO General Council is the most important of the three. The General Council is composed of all WTO members and oversees the main issues of the WTO: GATT, GATS, TRIPS, GATS. The General Council can form two other bodies.

The Dispute Settlement Body (DSB) is composed of panels that investigate complaints and adjudicate trade disputes. The Trade Policy Review Body (TPRB) reviews member trade policies and ensures that others are notified if policies are being enforced. The TPRB and DSB both report to the ministerial conference.

clearly	정의된	initial	조사
defined	시간표	consultation	상담
timetables	명확하게	last	지속
complete	완료	investigate	초기의

Unlike GATT, the WTO Dispute Settlement system is based on clearly defined rules, with timetables for completing cases.

- ***What was the Ministerial Conference?***
- ***What were the TPRB and DSB?***

At the longest, a case should not normally take more than one year. The different stages are as follows: The initial consultation period lasts 60 days. Then a panel of three experts investigate for six months.

appeal	제재	RTA	지역 무역 협정
stage	단계	dependency	지지하다
implementation	실행	major	의존
sanction	호소	support	주요

This is followed by an appeal stage and then, if the panel decides, implementation of sanctions. The WTO dealt with many issues that were not addressed by GATT, such as intellectual property, investment, services, and agriculture.

- ***Describe the WTO dispute settlement procedure.***
- ***Compared to GATT, which issues did the WTO address?***

Chapter

15 The Rise of Regional Trade Agreements

The creation of the WTO was one response to difficult trade negotiations under GATT. Another response was the rise of regionalism and regional trade agreements. The U.S. also supported the rise of RTAs. This chapter examines the rise of regional trade agreements and discusses Realist, Liberal, and Dependency explanations for the rise of RTAs, exploring the politics behind the creation of the E.U. Following World War Two, the major trading nations strongly supported multilateral trade liberalization

formation	지역주의	flow	통합
regionalism	성립	integration	제거하다
term	지리적	eliminate	흐름
geographic	기간	FTA	자유 무역 협정

• ***What do GATT and the rise of regionalism have in common?***

with the formation of the GATT (the General Agreement on Tariffs and Trade). Regionalism also emerged as a significant force in the postwar international trade system through the formation of regional trade agreements (RTAs).

15.1 Stages of Regional Integration

What is Regionalism? The term regionalism describes countries in a geographic region reducing barriers to the flow of trade, capital, and people. There are different stages of regional economic integration. The most basic RTA is the free trade area. A free trade area only eliminates barriers to trade between member countries. Each member of the FTA maintains separate trade policies toward non-member nations.

Customs Union	자유롭게	move	경제 연합
adopt	관세 동맹	Economic Union	통화
Common Market	공동 시장	currency	일치시키다
freely	채택하다	harmonization	이동

- ***What is regionalism?***
- ***What is a free trade area?***
- ***What is a customs union?***
- ***What is a common market?***
- ***What is an economic union?***
- ***What is a political union?***

A customs union requires more integration. The customs union eliminates barriers to trade between members, but also adopts a common trade policy toward non-member nations. Next, a common market is similar to a customs union, but it also allows people and capital to freely move between member countries. An economic union requires even closer integration.

An economic union includes establishment of a common currency and the harmonization

tax rate	논리적	fiscal policy	통화 정책
Political Union	세율	common	통화 정책
logical	정치 연합	monetary policy	차원
culmination	최고점	dimensions	공동

of tax rates. The final stage of integration is political union. It is the logical culmination of economic integration. It would lead to common fiscal policy as well as common monetary policy.

RTAs have grown in two dimensions:

deepening	제한	environmental	부흥되다
widening	불필요한	standard	휴면기에 있던
restriction	확대	dormant	기준
unnecessary	심화	revive	환경

- ***What are the two dimensions in which RTAs have grown?***
- ***How did RTAs deepen?***
- ***How did RTAs widen?***

deepening and widening. RTAs have deepened and become more fully integrated. They first eliminated trade restrictions by lowering tariffs and quotas. RTAs then eliminated other barriers to trade such as unnecessary health and environmental standards. They lowered barriers to trade in services, intellectual property, and investment.

RTAs also widened by including new member countries. New RTAs were established and dormant ones were revived. For instance, Mercosur and the Central American Common Market, which were founded in 1960, went dormant, and were then revived in 1993.

waves of	자연 산물	formation	동기
occur	생기다	EFTA	자극하다
phenomenon	물결	stimulate	형성
natural product	현상	motivation	유럽자유무역연합

15.2 The First Wave of Regional Integration

There have been two major waves of regionalism in the postwar period. The first wave of RTAs took place in the 1950s and 1960s. The second wave has occurred since the mid-1980s. Regional integration, though, is not a new phenomenon. A few older examples include a customs treaty among German states

---

• ***Which factors motivated the first wave of RTAs?***

in 1833 and the lifting tariffs on natural products between the U.S. and Canada in 1854.

Modern regional integration did not develop until the European Union after World War Two. The first wave of regionalism began with the formation of the European Community in 1957 and European Free Trade Association (EFTA) in 1960. European agreements stimulated the spread of regionalism throughout Latin America and Africa in the 1960s. The motivations for regionalism

reach	수입대체 산업화	dispute	제 3 세계
economies of scale	규모의 경제	relocate	이전하다
ISI	이르다	Third World	논쟁
fail	실패	fierce	맹렬한

included a search for larger markets, the desire to reach economies of scale for production of industrial goods, and the use of RTAs as part of an import substitution industrialization (ISI) plan. Most of these RTA plans failed outside of Europe. Several factors led to numerous disputes among RTA member states outside of Europe. Few industries wanted to relocate to the Third World, competition between developing countries was too fierce,

unequally	다자간	significant	오래 지속 되다
endorse	불평등하게	durable	크게
multilateral	침체되다	deepened	채택
stagnate	지지하다	adoption	심화로

And the benefits of these RTAs were distributed very unequally. Finally, the U.S. refused to endorse RTAs.

15.3 The Second Wave of Regional Integration

The U.S. instead supported multilateral free trade agreements. RTAs stagnated until a more significant second wave of regionalism. The second, more durable wave started in the mid-1980s, within and outside of Europe. The second wave began with the European Community (EC) increasing its membership and deepening integration. Spain and Portugal joined in 1986, and Austria, Finland and Sweden joined in 1995. The Europeans deepened integration with the adoption of a single market in 1992 and signing of the Maastricth Treaty, which created the European Union and the Euro as a common currency.

revive	설립	active	활동적인
liberalism	증가	barrier	완전히
proliferate	부흥	entirely	제거하다
establishment	자유주의	eliminate	장벽

- ***Why did the first wave of RTAs mostly fail outside of Europe?***
- ***Where did the second wave of RTAs begin?***

The U.S. which had long refused to join RTAs, began to join RTAs beginning in the mid-1980s. RTAs revived as well among developing countries. This time, unlike the 1960s, RTAs opened developing country markets to liberalism and global market forces. The number of RTAs rapidly proliferated. From the WTO's establishment in 1995, the number of active RTAs increased from 50 to 300. The WTO allowed FTAs and customs unions if they did not raise barriers to non-member countries, and entirely eliminated tariffs on trade between member nations.

report	이득	scale	규모
long term	보고하다	demand	다국간주의
voluntary	자발적인	multilateralism	수요
benefit	장기간	second best choice	차선책

WTO members are also required to report RTAs to the WTO.

- ***For developing nations, how did the second wave of RTAs differ from the first?***
- ***Does the WTO allow FTAs?***

15.4 Theoretical Explanations for the Rise of Regionalism

The three main theories of International Political Economy provide different explanations for the rise of RTAs.

15.41 The Liberal View

In contrast to Realists and Marxists, Liberals see RTAs as long term, voluntary deals that benefit all members. All member countries benefit, even though all might not equally benefit. Liberals argue that small states can gain through RTAs too. Their small power doesn't prevent them from benefitting, since they can gain by selling into a larger market. RTAs provide small states the opportunity to increase scale of production and gain economics of scale, and increase demand for their exports. While liberals consider WTO multilateralism the best way to liberalize trade, RTAs are a good second best choice.

suboptimal	협상
avoid	피하다
negotiating	달려 있다
depends	최적 이하의

create	자극하다
divert	전문화하다
stimulate	창출
specialize	전환

Although RTAs have fewer members, which Liberals consider suboptimal, this allows member countries to avoid the higher negotiating costs of the WTO.

• *Do small states gain from RTAs according to Liberals?*

Liberal support for RTAs depends on how much they increase trade and economic efficiency, which can be unclear since RTAs both create trade and divert trade. Liberals like the trade creation resulting from an RTA. More trade between member countries can stimulate economic growth, and trade leads countries to specialize

efficiently	생산자
lower cost	값이 더싼 생산자
producer	효율적으로
grain	곡물

barriers	보통
usually	장벽
rather	블록
bloc	보다

in the goods they most efficiently produce.

Trade diversion, however, reduces efficiency. Trade is diverted when the RTA favors less efficient producers inside the region over lower cost producers outside the region. An example of trade diversion would be E.U. member nations buying grain from high cost European producers, in France for instance, rather than from a lower cost producer in Canada. The amount of trade diversion depends on how high barriers are with non-member nations. Liberal economists, such as Lawrence and Krugman found that RTA efficiency gains are usually larger than costs from diversion.

The following factors make it more likely for RTAs to create trade rather than divert trade:

• ***What is trade creation and trade diversion?***

1) RTA members keep low trade barriers with non-member nations.

2) The RTA trade bloc is large.

close	근접해 있는
geographic	상호의존성
proximity	지리적
interdependence	가깝게

revival	개선 시키다
promote	촉진하다
attract	부흥
upgrade	유치

3) There was much trade between the RTA members before the agreement.

4) The RTA members are in close geographic proximity.

Krugman found that RTAs promote efficiency because most agreements were between geographic neighbors who traded with each other before the RTA.

How do Liberals explain the rise of RTAs? Liberals see increasing economic interdependence as a major factor in the revival of regionalism in the 1980s. States wanted to liberalize their economies to promote exports, attract foreign investment, and upgrade their technology.

• ***Which factor makes an RTA more likely to divert trade than create trade?***

demand	촉진하다	similar	현실 주의자
interest group	요구	interests	이해
transaction cost	이익 단체	satisfy	만족시키다
promote	거래 비용	Realist	유사

Important industries and firms were demanding liberalization, but multilateral institutions, like the GATT and WTO were not very effective. Too many nations and too many different interest groups raised the transaction costs of negotiations. So, in the liberal view, states promoted regionalism a second best method for increasing trade. Negotiation costs were lower with smaller groups of similar states. RTA members usually had similar income and development levels. Their similar interests were easier to satisfy through regional trade agreements.

15.42 The Realist View

Realists view RTAs differently and argue that the larger country in an RTA will gain more than a smaller country.

access	얻다	access	천연 자원
obtain	양보	natural resources	관계
NAFTA	접근	integration	접근
concession	북미 자유 무역 협정	relationships	통합

Realists argue that small countries must pay a high price for market access and to obtain economies of scale. The Realists refer to the example of NAFTA. Canada and Mexico wanted access to the large U.S. market. In return, the U.S. demanded concessions from Canada and Mexico in the areas of foreign investment, trade in services, and in access to natural resources, especially energy.

What is the cause of RTAs according to Realists? The economic integration of Western European in the first wave was a response to changes in the global power relationships.

emergence	출현	focus	보안
superpower	협력	security	식민지
facilitate	촉진하다	colony	영향
cooperation	초강대국	influence	초점

The emergence of the Soviet Union and the U.S. as superpowers facilitated cooperation among the Western States. Europeans could focus on economic integration because the USSR and the U.S. took responsibility for security. European countries had lost their colonies. The U.S. and the USSR were large countries, so the Europeans realized that integration was necessary to gain international influence.

- ***How do liberals explain the rise in RTAs?***
- ***For Realists who gains from RTAs: small states or big states? Why?***

recovery	회복
defend	원조금
OEEC	방어
aid	유럽 경제 협력기구

funds	통화
currency	자유화하다
convertible	교환
liberalize	자금

The U.S. supported integration to speed Western Europe economic recovery to defend against the Soviet threat. The U.S. supported the formation of Organization for European Economic Cooperation (OEEC) in 1948 to distribute Marshall Aid funds, to make the European currencies convertible, and to liberalize trade in Western Europe.

ECSC	방지
prevent	경쟁
renew	갱신
rivalry	유럽 석탄 철강 공동체

common	유럽 경제 공동체
EEC	다극
bipolar	양극
multipolar	공동

In 1951, Belgium, France, West Germany, Italy, Luxembourg and Netherlands formed the European Coal and Steel Community (ECSC) to prevent France and Germany from renewing their rivalry. It created a common market for coal and steel. Seven years later, the six countries formed the European

---

- ***According to Realists, how did Western European nations view the first wave of regionalization in Europe?***
- ***According to Realists, how did the US view the first wave of regionalization in Europe?***

Economic Community (EEC).

Realists think a shift in global distribution of power led to the second wave of RTAs. There was a change from a bipolar to a multipolar international system.

accept	지도력	deterrence	붕괴
leadership	받아들다	protection	독립적으로
depend	의존하다	demise	억지력
nuclear	핵	independently	보호

In the bipolar system, Western Europe and Japan accepted U.S. leadership. They depended on U.S. nuclear deterrence and economic assistance for protection against the Soviets. With the demise of the U.S.S.R. and of bipolarity, U.S. allies were willing to act independently of the U.S.

emergence	주요	hegemony	유지하다
major	출현	public good	패권
bloc	연합	maintain	공공재
decline	쇠퇴	regain	되찾다

This led to the emergence of three major regional economic blocs in Europe, North America, and East Asia and led to the relative decline of U.S. economic hegemony. As

---

- ***Why did Belgium, France, West Germany, Italy, Luxembourg and the Netherlands form the ECSC?***
- ***According to Realists, what led to the second wave of RTAs?***

American economic power declined, the U.S. was less willing to provide public goods by maintaining an open multilateral trade system. The U.S. sought to regain some of its economic power by joining RTAs, like NAFTA, in which US market power was strongest.

inaccurate	제거	unity	채택
removal	감축	competition	막다
decrease	정확 하지 않다	block	단일성
motivation	동기	adoption	경쟁

Some Realist predictions have been inaccurate though. Some Realists predicted that removal of the Soviet threat to Western Europe would decrease motivation for European unity. Some Realists predicted that increased competition between European states would block European integration. The adoption of the Euro as a common currency showed that this prediction was incorrect.

alternative	다국적기업	poorest	둘 수 있게 하다
rise	수혜자	industrial states	공업국
MNC	대안적	locate	가장 가난한
beneficiaries	출현	standards	기준

- ***Why did American interests towards regionalism change after the Cold War?***

15.43 The Marxist View

Marxists provide an alternative explanation for the rise of RTAs. Marxists argue that Multi-National Corporations (MNCs) and international capitalists are the main beneficiaries of RTAs. M.N.C.s are also the main beneficiaries of the E.U. and N.A.F.T.A.. Marxists argue that the main losers are the working class and the poorest people within industrial states and third world states. RTAs allow multinational corporations to locate production in states with low wages, bad environmental standards, and low taxes.

freely	수단	periphery	정의하다
region	자유롭게	revival	세력 균형
means	착취하다	define	주변
exploit	지역	balance of power	부흥

Multinational corporations can then freely export to other states in the region. RTAs are a means through which advanced states in the core can exploit developing states in the periphery.

In the Marxist view, the revival of RTAs in the 1980s was the result of increasingly powerful multinational corporations and international capital.

So, in summary, this chapter has defined and examined different types of regionalism, and compared the Realist, Liberal

---

- ***Were Realists correct that predicted that the end of the cold war would block European integration?***

and Dependency explanations for regionalism. Liberals see regionalism as an easier way to negotiate for free trade. Realists argue that changes in the balance of power led to the rise of regionalism. Dependency scholars claim that RTAs resulted from the power of M.N.C.s.

- ***According to Marxists, who are the main winners from RTAs?***
- ***According to Marxists, who are the main losers from RTAs***
- ***What is the Marxist explanation for RTAs?***

Chapter

16 Conclusion

perspective	가하다	insulated	우선순위
constraint	국가통제주의자	emanate	보호
imposed	관점	priorities	에서 나오다
statist	제한	deal with	대처하다

The book has examined domestic societal, domestic institutional and international approaches to international trade policy. Scholars who take an international perspective emphasize the constraints imposed on states by the global geo-strategic and diplomatic environment. They focus on the inherent conflict among states in a world in which cooperation is difficult to achieve.

Scholars who take a domestic approach differ by looking inside the nation state for explanations of international trade policy. Scholars taking a statist, or domestic institutionalist perspective, view the state as relatively insulated from the many political and economic pressures emanating from society. National leaders, policymakers and the political institutions within which they operate are seen as the main actors determining national priorities and implementing policies, including those dealing with foreign trade.

proponent	도구	determinant	에 근거하여
transmitter	근본	demand	결정 요인
underlying	전달자	radically	급진적으로
tool	지지자	on the basis of	수요

The opposing, domestic societal perspective focuses on economic and sociopolitical actors rather than political leaders. Proponents of the societal view minimize international constraints and view policymakers as little more than the transmitters of underlying societal demands. The state is seen as merely a tool of socioeconomic and political interests. Accordingly the determinants of national policy, including trade policy, are the demands made by individuals, firms, and groups rather than the independent actions of policymakers.

broaden	영향	subsidy	차별 없는
impact	넓어지다	nondiscriminatory	포함하다
encompass	포함하다	encompass	사멸하다
volume	용량	demise	보조금

These three views can be applied to help understand the

possible reversal to a long period of globalization, a process that involved the broadening and deepening of interactions and interdependence among societies and states throughout the world. While the domestic societal approach analyzes the effect of globalization on important groups within society, the international approach examines the impact of shifts in the global distribution of power on the powerful state's interests regarding globalization.

From 1980 to the present globalization extended geographic links to encompass virtually all major states so that policies adopted in one part of the world had a major impact on distant locations. Globalization also increased the frequency and intensity of interactions and interdependence among societies and states.

Under globalization the daily volume of foreign exchange trading in currencies rose from about $1 billion in the mid-1970s to $5.1 trillion in 2016, while foreign direct investment (FDI) flows rose from 55 billion in 1985 to $1.5 trillion in 2015 and global trade grew over twentyfold in the postwar period to $5.8 trillion in 2018. Advances in technology sharply reduced communications costs through telephone and the internet and transportation costs through containerization and air travel.

With globalization state policies that had traditionally been considered as domestic began to significantly impact other states, while traditionally "domestic" factors such as competition policies, subsidies, and financial market activity became subject to international regulation. MNCs, which played a central role in generating foreign direct investment, trade, and technology, pressed for nondiscriminatory trade and investment rules so that they could operate without restrictions abroad, and these new rules restricted the policymaking autonomy of nation-states.

The capitalist economic system grew to encompass the entire globe, with LDCs becoming more actively involved in the global economy and the formerly centrally planned economies of Eastern Europe and the former Soviet Union liberalizing their economies after the demise of communism. Major international economic organizations such as the International Monetary Fund (IMF), the World Bank, and the World Trade Organization (WTO) became global in scope.

wither	매력	stagnation	승선
appeal	비교할 수 있는	embark	공포감 조성 행위
fluctuate	시들다	sever	정체
comparable	변동	fear monger	절단하다

Globalization did not cause the state to wither away, though, and states adopted new and more complex functions to deal with an interdependent world. Some states responded to domestic group's appeals for assistance in dealing with global competitive pressures by resorting to trade protectionism, others adopted industrial policies to promote competitiveness, and still others allowed the market to function without interference.

Globalization is not unique to the present, and the internationalization of finance, trade, and production has fluctuated throughout history. Before World War I there was a high degree of interdependence in trade, foreign investment, and exports as a share of gross domestic product were comparable to present levels, while the migration of people around the world was even more extensive than today. The interdependent linkages of the nineteenth and early twentieth centuries virtually collapsed from increased nationalism and the Great Depression, however. Only after World War II did global economic ties begin to increase again.

16.1 The End of Globalization?

Rise of protectionism represented by the Trump 2016 election and Brexit and stagnation of international trade and investment may be a signal that the age of globalization is reaching an end. After his 2016 election, Donald Trump withdrew the U.S. from the 12 nation free trade Trans-Pacific Partnership, embarked on trade wars with China, Canada, Mexico and the EU, attacked Latino and Muslim immigrants and railed against "the ideology of globalism." The 2016 Brexit referendum for Britain to sever ties with the EU was built on the demand to "take back control" and fear mongering about refugees and immigrants.

decry	엄청나게	clout	분열되다
fuel	유지하다	undervalue	시나리오치
sentiment	감상	split	영향력
vastly	비난하다	scenario	과소평가하다

Similar movements decrying globalization also manifested in the Philippines, Turkey, Hungary, Poland, possibly France.

As political movements for protectionism have increased, the global trade of goods and services, as well as cross-border capital flows, which rose sharply as a share of global GDP throughout the 1990s and 2000s, began to level off from 2010.

Domestic societal theories of trade, in particular the factors model, can help explain the rise of anti-globalization throughout the industrialized world. As predicted, free trade benefited the abundant factor of production, which was capital and skilled labor in advanced nations and unskilled labor in developing countries, while driving down wages for unskilled workers in advanced democracies. While globalization enabled hundreds of millions to escape poverty, it increased wealth inequalities, eroded job security, stagnant wages, and jobs redundancies in industries like manufacturing, and turned middle- and lower-income households in developed economies against globalization. Immigration also threatened national identity, fueling resentment and anti-global sentiment.

From the international perspective, the rise of China

and waning of American hegemony may be the cause of globalization's decline. While China has vastly increased its economic strength and military clout through exports and attracting foreign capital and high technology under globalization, the US has grown weary of its strategic competitor's relative gains. The American government has accused the Chinese of intentionally undervaluing the Yuan to accumulate trade surpluses and of demanding that MNCs transfer American high technology in order to gain access to the Chinese market. The Trump administration has responded to the growing Chinese challenge by enacting steep tariffs on imports of Chinese goods, ushering in a US-China trade war.

What will the end of globalization look like? De-globalization could lead to a mild form of regionalization, in which production is clustered in neighboring countries rather than globalized, or in an extreme case could split the world into competing blocs, in which one is led by the U.S. and another by China. Under this scenario, trade and investment flows between the West and China would dry up completely, in a repeat of the Cold War between the U.S. and the former Soviet Union. A mix of restrictions on trade in specific sectors and products seems more likely, as does increasing restrictions on the transfer of high technology.

Domestic Politics and International Relations

Cohn, Theodore H., and Patrick J. Smith. "Subnational Governments as International Actors: Constituent Diplomacy in the Pacific Northwest." *BC Studies* 110 (Summer 1996): 25-59.

Cox, Ronald W. *Power and Profits: U.S. Policy in Central America*. Lexington, KY: University Press of Kentucky, 1994.

Eichengreen, Barry. *The Gold Standard and the Great Depression, 1919-1939*. New York: Oxford University Press, 1992.

Gourevitch, Peter. "The Second Image Reversed: The International Sources of Domestic Politics." *International Organization* 32-4 (Autumn 1978): 881 -912.

Ikenberry, G. John. "The Irony of State Strength: Comparative Responses to the Oil Shocks in the 1970s." *International Organization* 40 -1(Winter1986): 105-137.

Katzenstein, Peter J. "International Relations and Domestic Structures: Foreign Economic Policies of Advanced Industrial States." *International Organization* 30-1(Winter 1976): 1-45.

Keohane, Robert and Helen V. Milner, eds. *Internationalization and Domestic Politics*. Cambridge, UK: Cambridge University Press, 1996.

Milner, Helen V. R*esisting Protectionism: Global Industries and the Politics of International Trade*. Princeton, NJ: Princeton University Press, 1988.

Putnam, Robert D. "Diplomacy and Domestic Politics: The Logic of Two-Level Games." *International Organization* 42 (Summer 1988): 427-460.

Simmons, Beth A. *Who Adjusts? Domestic Sources of Foreign Economic Policy during the Interwar Years*. Princeton, NJ: Princeton University Press, 1994.

Hegemonic Stability Theory

Cowhey, Peter F., and Edward Long. "Testing Theories of Regime Change: Hegemonic Decline or Surplus Capacity?" *International Organization* 37-2 (Spring 1983): 157-188.

Huntington, Samuel P. "Transnational Organizations in World Politics." *World Politics* 25-3 (April 1973): 333-368.

Kennedy, Paul. *The Rise and fall of the Great Powers: Economic Change and Military Conflict from 1500 to 2000*. New York: Random House, 1987.

Keohane, Robert. *After Hegemony: Cooperation and Discord in the World Political Economy*. Princeton, NJ: Princeton

University Press, 198

Kindleberger, Charles P. *The World in Depression, 1929-1939*. Berkeley, CO: University of California Press, 1973.

Nau, Henry R. *The Myth of America's Decline: Leading the World Economy into the 1990s*. New York: Oxford University Press, 1990.

Nye, Joseph S., Jr. "Soft Power." *Foreign Policy* 80 (Fall 1990): 153-171.

Olson, Mancur. *The Logic of Collective Action: Public Goods and the Theory of Groups*. Cambridge, MA: Harvard University Press, 1965.

Russett, Bruce. "The Mysterious Case of Vanishing Hegemony; or, Is Mark Twain Really Dead?" *International Organization* 39-2 (Spring 1985): 207-231.

Snidal, Duncan. "The Limits of Hegemonic Stability Theory." *International Organization* 39-4 (Autumn 1985): 579-61

Stein, Arthur A. "The Hegemon's Dilemma: Great Britain, the United States and the International Economic Order." *International Organization* 38-2 (Spring 1984): 355-386.

Strange, Susan. "The Future of the American Empire." *Journal of International Affairs* 42 (Fall 1988): 1-17.

Thurow, Lester. *Head to Head: The Coming Economic Battle among Japan, Europe, and America*. New York: Morrow, 1992.

Webb, Michael C., and Stephen D. Krasner. "Hegemonic Stability Theory: An Empirical Assessment." *Review of*

International Studies 15 (Spring 1989): 183-198.

Zuckerman, Mortimer B. "A Second American Century." *Foreign Affairs* 77-3 (May/June,1998): 18-31.

International Institutions

Cohn, Theodore H. "The Changing Role of the United States in the Global Agricultural Trade Regime." *In World Agriculture and the CATT, International Political Economy Yearbook*, vol. 7, ed. William P. Avery, 17-38. Boulder, CO: Rienner, 1993.

Haggard, Stephan, and Beth A. Simmons. "Theories of International Regimes." *International Organization* 41-3 (Summer 1987): 491-517

Jacobson, Harold K. *Networks of Interdependence: International Organizations and the Global Political System*. New York: Knopf, 1979

Kahler, Miles. *International Institutions and the Political Economy of Integration*. Washington, DC: Brookings Institution, 1995

Keohane, Robert. *International Institutions and State Power: Essays in International Relations Theory*. Boulder, CO: Westview Press, 1989.

Krasner, Stephen D., ed. *International Regimes*. Ithaca, NY: Cornell University Press, 1983.

Martin, Lisa and Beth Simmons. "Theories and Empirical Studies ofInternational Institutions." *International Organization* 52-4 (Autumn 1998): 729-757.

Mearsheimer, John J. "The False Promise of International Institutions." *International Security* 19-3 (Winter 1994-95): 5-49.

Taylor, Phillip. *Nonstate Actors in International Politics: From Transregional to Substate Organizations*. Boulder, CO: Westview Press, 1984.

International Political Economy

Doyle, Michael W., and G. John Ikenberry. *New Thinking in International Relations Theory*. Boulder, CO: Westview Press, 1997.

Frieden, Jeffry A., and David A. Lake, eds. *International Political Economy: Perspectives on Global Power and Wealth*. New York: St. Martin's Press, 3rd edition, 1995.

Gerschenkron, Alexander. *Economic Backwardness in Historical Perspective*. Cambridge, MA.: Harvard University Press, 1962.

Gilpin, Robert, with Jean Gilpin. *The Political Economy of International Relations*. Princeton, NJ: Princeton University Press, 1987.

Kegley, Charles W., Jr., ed. *Controversies in International*

Relations Theory: Realism and the Neoliberal Challenge. New York: St. Martin's Press, 1995.

Kindleberger, Charles P. *Power and Money: The Economics of International Politics and the Politics of International Economics*. New York: Basic Books, 1970.

Lindblom, Charles E. *Politics and Markets: The World's Political-Economic Systems*. New York: Basic Books, 1977.

Olson, Mancur. *The Logic of Collective Action: Public Goods and the Theory of Groups*. Cambridge, MA: Harvard University Press, 1965.

Polanyi, Karl. *The Great Transformation*. Boston, MA: Beacon Press, 1965.

Strange, Susan. "International Economics and International Relations: A Case of Mutual Neglect." *International Affairs* 46 (April 1970): 304-315.

Webb, Michael C. *The Political Economy of Policy Coordination: International Adjustment since 1945*. Ithaca, NY: Cornell University Press, 1995.

Liberal Theory

Axelrod, Robert. *The Evolution of Cooperation*. New York: Basic Books, 1984.

Balassa, Bela, ed. *The Newly Industrializing Countries in the World Economy*. New York: Pergamon Press, 1981.

Cooper, Richard N. *The Economics of Interdependence: Economic Policy in the Atlantic Community*. New York: McGraw-Hill, 1968.

Friedman, Milton, ed. *Essays in Positive Economics*. Chicago, IL: University of Chicago Press, 1953.

Fukuyama, Francis. "The End of History?" *The National Interest* 16 (Summer 1989): 3-18.

Hall, Peter A., ed. *The Political Power of Economic Ideas: Keynesianism across Nations*. Princeton, NJ: Princeton University Press, 1989.

Hayek, F. A. *New Studies in Philosophy, Politics, Economics and the History of Ideas*. Chicago, IL: University of Chicago Press, 1978.

Keohane, Robert and Joseph S. Nye Jr., eds. *Power and Interdependence: World Politics in Transition*. Boston, MA: Little, Brown, 1977.

Keynes, John Maynard. *The General Theory of Employment, Interest, and Money*. New York: Harcourt, Brace and World, 1935.

Krasner, Stephen D., ed. *International Regimes*. Ithaca, NY: Cornell University Press, 1983.

Moravcsik, Andrew. "Taking Preferences Seriously: A Liberal Theory of International Politics." *International Organization* 51-4 (Autumn 1997): 513-553.

Oye, Kenneth A., ed. *Cooperation under Anarchy*. Princeton, NJ: Princeton University Press, 1986.

Ricardo, David. *The Principles of Political Economy and Taxation*. Homewood, IL: Irwin, 1963.

Risse-Kappen, Thomas, ed. *Bringing Transnational Relations Back In: Non-State Actors, Domestic Structures and International Institutions*. Cambridge, UK: Cambridge University Press, 1995.

Rostow, W. W. *The Stages of Economic Growth: A Non-Communist Manifesto*. Cambridge, UK: Cambridge University Press, 1960.

Smith, Adam. *The Wealth of Nations*. London: Dent & Sons, Everyman's Library, 1910.

Marxism and Dependency Theory

Caporaso, James. "Dependency Theory: Continuities and Discontinuities in Development Studies." *International Organization* 34-4 (Autumn 1980): 605-628.

Cardoso, Fernando Henrique. "The Consumption of Dependency Theory in the United States." *Latin American Research Review* 12-3 (1977): 7-24.

Cardoso, Fernando Henrique, and Enzo Faletto. *Dependency and Development in Latin America*. Translated by Marjory Mattingly Urquidi. Berkeley, CA: University of California Press, 1979.

Cox, Robert W. *Production, Power, and World Order: Social*

Forces in the Making of History. New York, NY: Columbia University Press, 1987.

De Vroey, Michel. "A Regulation Approach Interpretation of Contemporary Crisis." *Capital & Class* 23 (Summer 1984): 45-66.

Frank, Andre Gunder. *Capitalism and Underdevelopment in Latin America: Historical Studies of Chile and Brazil*. New York: Monthly Review Press, 1967.

Galtung, Johan. "A Structural Theory of Imperialism." *Journal of Peace Research* 8-2 (1971): 81-117.

Gereffi, Gary. *The Pharmaceutical Industry and Dependency in the Third World*. Princeton, NJ: Princeton University Press, 1983.

Gramsci, Antonio. *Selections from the Prison Notebooks of Antonio Gramsci*. Edited and translated by Quintin Hoare and Geoffrey Nowell Smith. New York: International Publishers, 1971.

Lenin, V. I. *Imperialism: The Highest Stage of Capitalism*. Revised translation. New York: International Publishers, 1939.

Marx, Karl, and Frederick Engels. *Selected Works*. New York: International Publishers, 1968.

Prebisch, Raul. *Towards a Dynamic Development Policy for Latin America*. New York: United Nations, 1963.

Skocpol, Theda. "'Wallerstein's World Capitalist System: A Theoretical and Historical Critique."*American Journal of*

Sociology 82-5 (March 1977): 1075-1090.

Valenzuela, J. Samuel, and Arturo Valenzuela. "Modernization and Dependency: Alternative Perspectives in the Study of Latin American Development." *Comparative Politics* 10 (July 1978): 535-557.

Wallerstein, Immanuel. *The Modem World System: Capitalist Agriculture and the Origins of the European World-Economy in the Sixteenth Century*. New York: Academic Press, 1974.

Multinational Corporations

Bergsten, C. Fred, and Marcus Noland. *Reconcilable Differences? United States-Japan Economic Conflict*. Washington, DC: Institute for International Economics, 1993.

Caves, Richard E. *Multinational Enterprise and Economic Analysis*. Cambridge, UK: Cambridge University Press, 2nd edition, 1996.

Gilpin, Robert. U.S. *Power and the Multinational Corporation: The Political Economy of Foreign Direct Investment*. New York: Basic Books, 1975.

Hertner, Peter, and Geoffrey Jones. *Multinationals: Theory and History*. Aldershot, UK: Gower, 1986.

Kindleberger, Charles P., and David B. Audretsch, eds. *The Multinational Corporation in the 1980s*. Cambridge, MA:

MIT Press, 1983.

Krugman, Paul. "Competitiveness: A Dangerous Obsession." *Foreign Affairs* (March/April 1994): 28-44.

Modelski, George, ed. *Transnational Corporations and World Order: Readings in International Political Economy*. San Francisco, CA: Freeman, 1979.

Moran, Theodore H., ed. *Multinational Corporations: The Political Economy of Foreign Direct Investment*. Lexington, MA: Heath, 1985.

Reich, Robert B. *The Work of Nations: Preparing Ourselves for Twenty-first Century Capitalism*. New York: Vintage Books, 1991.

Stopford, John M., and Susan Strange, with John S. Henley. Rival States, *Rival Firms: Competition for World Market Shares*. Cambridge, UK: Cambridge University Press, 1991.

Vernon, Raymond. *Sovereignty at Bay: The Multinational Spread of U. S. Enterprises*. New York: Basic Books, 1971.

Realist Theory

Evans, Peter B., Dietrich Rueschemeyer, and Theda Skocpol, eds. *Bringing the State Back In*. Cambridge, UK: Cambridge University Press, 1985.

Gilpin, Robert. *War and Change in World Politics*. Cambridge,

UK: Cambridge University Press, 1981.

Grieco, Joseph. *Cooperation among Nations: Europe, America, and Non-Tariff Barriers to Trade*. Ithaca, NY: Cornell University Press, 1990.

Hart, Jeffrey A. *The New International Economic Order: Conflict and Cooperation in North South Economic Relations, 1974-77*. London: Macmillan, 1983.

Hirschman, Albert. *National Power and the Structure of Foreign Trade*. Berkeley, CA: University of California Press, expanded edition, 1980.

Johnson, Chalmers. *MITI and the Japanese Miracle: The Growth of Industrial Policy, 1925-1975*. Stanford, CA: Stanford Url.versity Press, 1982.

Keohane, Robert ., ed. *Neorealism and Its Critics*. New York: Columbia University Press, 1986.

Krasner, Stephen D. *Defending the National Interest: Raw Materials Investments and U.S. Foreign Policy*. Princeton, NJ: Princeton University Press, 1978.

Lake, David A. "Power and the Third World: Toward a Realist Political Economy of North South Relations." *International Studies Quarterly* 31-2 (June 1987): 217-234.

List, Friedrich. *The National System of Political Economy*. Translated by Sampson S. Lloyd. London: Longmans, Green, 1916.

Machiavelli, Niccolo. *The Prince and the Discourses*. New York:

Modem Library, 1940.

Mastanduno, Michael, David A. Lake, and G. John Ikenberry, "Toward a Realist Theory of State Action." *International Studies Quarterly* 33-4 (December 1989): 457-474.

Morgenthau, Hans. J., revised by Kenneth W. Thompson. *Politics among Nations: The Struggle for Power and Peace*. New York: Knopf, 6th edition, 1985.

Syrett, Harold C., ed. *The Papers of Alexander Hamilton*, vol. 10. New York: Columbia University Press, 1966.

Thucydides. *The History of the Peloponnesian War*. Translated by Richard Crawley. London: Dent, Everyman's Library, 1963.

Waltz, Kenneth N. *Theory of International Politics*. Reading, MA: Addison Wesley, 1979.

Regionalism

Anderson, Kym, and Richard Blackhurst, eds. *Regional Integration and the Global Trading System*. Hertfordshire, UK: Harvester Wheatsheaf, 1993.

Balassa, Bela. *The Theory of Economic Integration*. London: Allen and Unwin, 1962.

Cable, Vincent, and David Henderson, eds. *Trade Blocs? The Future of Regional Integration*. London: Royal Institute of International Affairs, 1994.

Cohn, Theodore H. "Emerging Issues in Canada-U.S. Agricultural Trade Under the GATT and FTA." *Canadian-American Public Policy* no. 10. Orono, ME: University of Maine, Canadian American Center, June 1992.

Fischer, Thomas C. *The United States, the European Union, and the "Globalization" of World Trade*. Westport, CT: Quorum Books, 2000.

Haas, Ernst B. *The Obsolescence of Regional Integration Theory*. Berkeley, CA: University of California, Institute of International Studies, Research Series no. 25, 1975.

Kahler, Miles. *Regional Futures and Transatlantic Economic Relations*. New York: Council on Foreign Relations, 1995.

Keohane, Robert, and Stanley Hoffmann. *The New European Community: Decisionmaking and Institutional Change*. Boulder, CO: Westview Press, 1991.

Lipsey, R. G., and Kelvin Lancaster. "The General Theory of Second Best." *The Review of Economic Studies* 24-1(1956-57): 11-32.

Nader, Ralph. *The Case against 'Free Trade': GATT, NAFTA, and the Globalization of Corporate Power*. San Francisco, CA: Earth Island Press, 1993.

Schott, Jeffrey J., ed. Free *Trade Areas and U.S. Trade Policy*. Washington, DC: Institute for International Economics, 1989.

Viner, Jacob. *The Customs Union Issue*. New York: Carnegie

Endowment for International Peace, 1950.

World Trade Organization. *Regionalism and the World Trading System*. Geneva, Switzerland: World Trade Organization, April 1995.

Trade Relations

Aggarwal, V. K. *Liberal Protectionism: The International Politics of Organized Textile Trade*. Berkeley, CA: University of California Press, 1985.

Bhagwati, Jagdish. *The World Trading System at Risk*. New York: Harvester Wheatsheaf, 1991.

Cameron, James, and Karen Campbell, eds. *Dispute Resolution in the World Trade Organisation*. London: Cameron, 1998.

Cohn, Theodore H. *The International Politics of Agricultural Trade: Canadian-American Relations in a Global Agricultural Context*. Vancouver, Canada: University of British Columbia Press, 1990.

Conybeare, John A. C. *Trade Wars: The Theory and Practice of International Commercial Rivalry*. New York: Columbia University Press, 1987.

Curzon, Gerard. *Multilateral Commercial Diplomacy: The General Agreement on Tariffs and Trade and Its Impact on National Commercial Policies and Techniques*.

London: Michael Joseph, 1965.

Destler, I. M. *American Trade Politics*. Washington, DC: Institute for International Economics and The Twentieth Century Fund, 2nd edition, June 1992.

Haus, Leah A. *Globalizing the GATT: The Soviet Union's Successor States, Eastern Europe, and the International Trading System*. Washington, DC: Brookings Institution, 1992.

Higgott, Richard A., and Andrew Fenton Cooper. "Middle Power Leadership and Coalition Building: Australia, the Cairns Group, and the Uruguay Round of Trade Negotiations." *International Organization* 44-4 (Autumn 1990): 589-632.

Hirschman, Albert O. *National Power and the Structure of Foreign Trade*. Berkeley, CA: University of California Press, 1945.

Krasner, Stephen D. "State Power and the Structure of International Trade." *World Politics* 28 (April 1976): 317-347.

Lake, David A., *Power, Protection, and Free Trade: International Sources of U.S. Commercial Strategy, 1887-1939*. Ithaca, NY: Cornell University Press, 1988.

Odell, John S., and Thomas D. Willett. *International Trade Policies: Gains from Exchange between Economics and Political Science*. Ann Arbor, MI: University of Michigan Press, 1990.

GLOSSARY

A

abandon	폐지/버리다
abroad	해외
absence	부재
absent	결석
absolute	절대적인
Absolute advantage	절대 우위
absolute gain	절대 이득
absorb	흡수하다
abstract	추상적인
abundant	풍부한
abuse	남용
academia	학계
accept	받아들다
access	접근
accomplish	할수있다
accord with	일치
according to	에 따르면
account	차지하다
accumulation	축적
accuracy	정확성
achieve	달성
achieve	우위에 서다
Act	법안
action	행동
active	적극적인/활동적인
actor	행위자
actual	실제
ad hoc	즉석
address	처리/살펴 보다
adjudicate	판결하다
adjust	적응
adopt	채택하다
adult literacy	성인문해교육
advance	촉진
advanced nation	선진국
advances	진보
advantage	이점
advise	조언하다
advocate	옹호
affiliates	계열사
afford	여유
AFL	미국 노동 총연맹
agency	기관
aggressive	공격적인
agree	동의하다
agriculture	농업
aid	원조
aims	목적을 둔 것이다
airlines	항공사
airplane	비행기
align	제휴
alliance	동맹
allies	동맹국
allocate	할당
allowing	확장한
alternative	대안적
alternative policy	대안책
amend	개정하다
among	중
amount	양
analysis	분석
anarchy	무정부 상태

answer to	에 대하여 책임지지 않다
apparel	의류
apparently	분명히
appeal	이의를 제기/호소
appellate	상소
applicable	해당되는/적용 되다
approach	접근
arbitrarily	독단적으로 구축
argue	주장
arguments	논쟁
aristocrats	귀족
armaments	군비
arms race	군비 경쟁
arrange	정리하다
arrangement	협정
array	종류
Asiatic	아시아
aspects	측면
assembly	의회
assembly line	조립 라인
assistance	원조
association	협회
assumption	가정
at the expense	희생으로
at the same time	동시에
ATMI	미국 섬유 제조 협회
attack	비난
attorney	변호사
attract	유치
attractive	매력적인
authoritarian	권위주의적인
authority	권위
authorize	권한이 있다
automatically	자동적으로
automatically	자동적으로
autonomous	자율적
autonomy	자율성
autos	자동차
avert	막다
avoid	피하다

B

backwardness	후진성
balance of payments	국제수지
balance of power	세력 균형
balance of trade	무역 수지
balanced	균형이 잡힌
bank	은행
bankrupt	파산한
bargaining	흥정
barrier	장벽
base	기지
based	기반으로
basic	기본
basically	근본적으로
basis	기초/근거
battle	전투
be able to	할 수 있다
be better off	더 나은 것입니다
be treated	취급 되다
bear costs	비용을 부담하다
been involved	참여했다
beforehand	사전에
beg	구걸
begun	시작
behavior	행동

belief	믿음
below market rate	시세보다 낮은
beneficiaries	수혜자
benefit	이득
benevolent	자애로운
betray	배신하다
better off	더 나은
beyond	이상으로
bias	편견
bilateral	양자간
binding	구속력
bio-technology	생물 기술
bipolar	양극
blame	비난을 받다
bloc	블록
block	저지/막다
body	기구
bolster	강화하다
bolt	필
border	경계
borrow	빌다
both countries	양국
bourgeoisie	자본가 계급
branch	지점/종류
break down	결렬되다
bridge	교량
bring about	가능해집니다
bring back	수출
broad	넓은
budget	예산
build	구축
built on to	보충
bureaucracy	관료제도
Business Roundtable	기업인 간담회
buy	사다
by default	자동적으로
by itself	스스로

C

capability	능력
capacity	수용력
capital	자본
capital market	자본시장
capital rich	자본이 풍부한
capital-intensive	자본 집약적
capitalism	자본주의
capitalist	자본가
capture	포획
care about	대해 생각하다
carry out	수행하다
case	케이스
catastrophic	치명적인
catch up	따라잡다
categorize	분류하다
cattle	가축
causal	원인이 되는
cautious	신중
cells	감방
center	중심
century	세기
CEO	최고 경영자
certain	특정
certified	공인
challenge	도전
chance	기회
characterize	특징있다

charter	헌장	Commerce Department	상무부
cheaply	싸게	commercial	상업의
cheating	속임수가	commission	위원회
chemical factory	화학 공장	committed	전념
chicken	치킨	committed to	옹호하다
chief	최고의	committee	위원회
Christian	기독교도	commodity	상품
CIO	산업별 조합회의	common	흔한
circuit board	회로 기판	Common Market	공동 시장
circuits	회로	communications	통신
circumstance	환경	communism	공산주의
circumvent	피하다	communities	공동체들
citizen	시민	comparative	비교적
city state	도시 국가	comparative advantage	비교 우위
civil servant	공무원	compensation	보상
civil war	내전	compete	경쟁하다
claim	주장하다/청구	competition	경쟁
class	계급	competitive	경쟁력있는
clause	약관	complainant	제기하는 국가
clear	명확한	complaint	불만
close	가깝게/긴밀한	complete	완결하다/완료
closely	긴밀히	completely	완전히
club	클럽	complicate	더 복잡하게되다
coal	석탄	comply	따르다
coalition	연합	component	장비
code	코드/규칙	composed of	구성
coercive	강압적	comprehension	이해력
coincide	동시에	comprehensive	포괄적
Cold War	냉전	comprise	구성된
collapse	붕괴되다	compromise	타협
collective	집단	computer	컴퓨터
Collective Action	집단 행동	concede	인정하다
collude	결탁	concentrate	집중
colonies	식민지	concerned	걱정하는

concerned with 관련된
concession 양보
concessional 양허성
conditions 조건
conducive 도움이되는
conduct 지휘 하에 있다
confer 주다
Conference 회의
confession 고백
confidence 확신
confirm 확인하다
conflict 충돌/분쟁
Confucianism 유교
Congressional 의회
consensus 일치
consequence 결과
Conservatism 보수주의
consistent 일치하는
consistently 지속적으로
constant 일정한
constituency 선거구
constituted 구성된
constrain 제한
construct 만들다
consultation 상담
consume 소비하다/소모하다
consumer 소비자
consumption 소비
contentious 논쟁적인
context 속에서
contexts 문맥
contract 계약
contrast 차이/반면에
contrasted 대조
contribute 공헌/지불
control 통제/제어
controversial 논란이 많다
convert 변환
convertible 교환
conviction 유죄선고
convince 납득시키다
cooperate 협력하다
copy 본받다
core 핵심
Corn Law 곡물조령
correct 적당한
correlate 연관성이 있음
cost 비용
costless 비용이없는
costs per unit 단가
council 회의
counter 반박
counteract 중화하
countervailing 상계
cover 적용
CPU 중앙 처리 장치
craft 설립하다
crash 충돌
create 만들다/창출
credit 신용
crisis 위기
critic 비평가
criticism 비판
crop 농작물
cross 넘나들다
culmination 최고점
cultural 문화적
currency 통화

customs tax	관세
Customs Union	관세 동맹
cut	끝내는 것
cut down	잘라
cut off	차단
cutting edge	첨단 기술이

D

dairy	낙농
danger	위험
data processing	자료처리기
deal with	다루다/처리
debt	채무/부채
debtor	채무자
decade	10년
decades	수십 년
decent	괜찮은
decline	쇠퇴
decrease	감축
deduce	추론하다
deepened	심화로
defect	배반
defense	방어/국방
defense spending	국방 지출
deficits	적자
define	정의하다
defined	정의된
definitively	확실하게
degree	정도
delays	지연
delegate	위임
demand	수요/필요
demise	붕괴
democracy	민주주의
Democratic Party	민주당
demonstrate	시위
deny	거부
depend	의존하다
Dependency	의존
Dependent variable	종속 변수
depends	달려 있다
deregulate	규제를 해제하다
description	설명
desirable	가치있는
desire	원하다
despite	에도 불구하다
destroy	파괴하다
determine	결정
deterrence	억지력
devalue	평가 절하하다
development	개발
differentiation	차별화
dilemma	고민
dimensions	차원
diplomatic	외교
direct	곧장
direction	방향
Director	이사인
disagreement	의견 차이
disappear	사라지다
discernible	뚜렷한
discipline	훈련
discourage	관행
discredit	신빙성이 없는
discriminate	차별하다
disguise	위장

dispute	논쟁/분쟁
distant	먼
distinct	명백
distortion	왜곡
distress	곤궁에 처해진
distributional	분배
district	선거구
divert	전환
divide	분열시키다
divide and rule	분할과 통치의 (각개격파)
division of labor	분담
doesn't care	상관하지 않다
domestic	국내
dominance	지배적인
dormant	휴면기에 있던
down the road	도로를 계속
downgrade	중요하지 않다고 생각하다
downturn	침체
drafted	구상하다
dramatic	극적인
draw on	사용하다
dumping	덤핑
durable	오래 지속 되다/내구
duties	관세
dynamic	역동적

E

each stage	각 단계
earn	얻다
ecology	환경
Economic Union	경제 연합
economies of scale	규모의 경제
economist	경제학자
ECSC	유럽 석탄 철강 공동체
educated	교육받은
education	교육
EEC	유럽 경제 공동체
effective	효과적인
EFTA	유럽자유무역연합
egalitarian	평등
elect	선출하다
electoral district	선거구
electronics	전자 제품
element	요소
eliminate	제거하다
elite	엘리트
embrace	받아들이다
emerge	떠올라다/출현
emergency loans	긴급 대출
emotional	감정적
emphasize	강조하다
empire	제국
empirical	실제적
employ	고용
employee	직원
employment	고용
empower	권한을 부여하다
empty threat	공허한 협박
emulate	본받다
enacted	제정
enclave	고립된
encounter	겪다
encourage	하도록 하다/격려하다
encouraged	격려
endorse	지지하다
endowment	부존

enforce	집행
engage	채택
engaging in	에 참여
engine	엔진
enhance	강화
enormous	엄청난
ensure	확실히/보장
entire	전체
entirely	완전히
entrepreneur	사업가
entrepreneurship	기업 정신
entry	진입
environmental	환경
EOI	수출지향적인 산업화
equal	되는건
equalize	똑같아 지다
equally	동등하게
escape	벗어나다
especially	특히
established	확실히 자리를 잡은
establishment	설립
EU	유럽 연합
European Community	유럽 공동체
evade	피하다
evaluate	평가하다
evidence	증거
evolution	진화
exacerbate	악화시키다
exaggerate	과장하다
examine	검토
example	예
exception	예외
excess	초과
exchange	교환
exchange rate	환율
exclude	제외하다
executive branch	행정부
exemptions	면제
exercise	발휘
exist	존재하다
existence	존재
expand	확대
expansion	확장
expense	지출
experience	경험
explanation	설명
explicit	명백한
exploit	착취하다
export	수출
export-led	수출 주도
external	외부
externality	외부효과
extra	여분의
extract	추출

F

fabrication	제조
facilitate	촉진하다
facility	시설
facing	직면
factor	요인/요소
factors of production	생산 요소
factory	공장
fail	실패
fairly	공정하다
fairness	공정성

falls	줄입니다
family based	가족 기반
family ties	가족의 유대
famine	기근
famous	유명한
farmer	농부
fascinated	관심을 갖다
fast enough	빨리
fast track	빠른 길
favor	선호
favorable	유리한
FDI	해외 직접 투자
fear	두려움은
fell	떨어졌다
fertilizer	비료
feudalism	봉건 제도
few	많지 않은
fewer	적어지다
fierce	맹렬한
figure	인물
finance	금융
financial	재정
Find out	알아내다
finished	완성
finished advanced goods	고급 완성품
fire	해고
firm	회사
first glance	첫눈에
first mover	맨 먼저 움직이는 사람
fiscal policy	통화 정책
fixed tax	고정 세
flat	평면
flexibility	유연성이/융통성
flow	흐름
focus	초점
following way	다음과 같은 방법
footwear	신발
for instance	예를 들어
force	강요하다/하도록 강요
force down	강제 하향 조절
foregone	포기했던
foreign aid	대외 원조
foreign exchange	외환
foreign investment	해외 투자
foreigners	외국인
forgo	가하지 않다
form	수립
formal	공식적인
format	구성 방식
formation	성립/형성
former	전
foundation	기초
framework	가정
free from	으로부터 자유롭게
Free markets	자유 시장
free ride	무임 승차
Free trader	자유무역 지지자
freely	자유롭게
frontier days	개척시대
frozen	얼어
FTA	자유 무역 협정
full employment	완전 고용
full information	완전한 정보
full-fledged	자격을 제대로 갖춘
function	기능
funds	자금
further	촉진

G

gain	이익
Game Theory	게임 이론
gap	격차
gasoline	휘발유
GATT	관세 및 무역에 관한 일반 협정
GDP	국내총생산
GEC	일반적인 제외 조항
general	일반
general public	대중
generate	만들다/창출/이르게 하다
genetically	유전자
genuine	진정한/진짜의
geographic	지리적
geography	지리학
get up to	할 수 있을 만큼
give up	포기하다
given	우리가 알고 있을 때
globalization	세계화
glove	장갑
GNP	국내총생산
goods	상품
grain	곡물
grain market	곡물 시장
grant	부여
Great Depression	대공황
groundwork	토대
grow up	성장
guide	인도
GVCs	글로벌가치사슬

H

habit	습관
handle	처리
hard work	노고
hardware	하드웨어
harm	해치다
harmonization	일치시키다
have to pay	지불해야 한다
head start	유리한 출발
health care industry	의료 산업
hear	듣다
heavily	많이 해
hegemon	패권국
help each other	서로 도와 줘
high demand	높은 수요
high skilled	숙련 된
high technology	첨단 기술
highly educated	고등 교육을 받은
hinder	방해하다
historical	역사적인
hold	보유/개최
hold back	가로막다
honesty	정직
host	유치하다
hotel industry	호텔 산업
House of Commons	하원
House of Lords	상원
House of Representatives	하원
household	가정
hundred thousand	십만
hypothesis	가설

I

identical	동일한
identify	식별하다
identify	식별
ideological	이념적
ideology	사상
ignore	무시하다
imagine	상상하다
imbalance	불균형
IMF	국제 통화 기금
immediately	즉시
impact	영향
impede	방해하다
impediment	장애물
imperial	제국
imperialism	제국주의
implement	시행하다
implementation	실행
Import	수입
impose	가하다
imprisonment	보내다
improvement	향상
in circulation	사용되다
in comparison	비교하여
in line with	와 같은
in place	체재하다
in return	그 대가로
in summary	요약하자면
in the long run	장기적으로는
in turn	결국
inaccurate	정확 하지 않다
inadequate	부적당
inappropriate	부적절한
inattention	무관심
incentive	동기
include	포함
income	소득
incorporated	이뤄지는 것
indebted	빚이 많은
Independent variable	독립 변수
independently	독립적으로
indicate	나타나다
industrial	산업
industrial base	산업 기반
industrial policy	산업 정책
industrial sector	산업 부문
industrial states	공업국
industrialization	산업화
industrialized	산업화된
inefficient	비효율적인
inequality	불평등
inevitable	피할 수 없는
infamous	악명 높은
infant	유치
infant industries	유치산업
inflation	인플레이션
inflow	유입
influence	영향력
informal	비공식
information technology	정보 기술
infrastructure	사회 기반 시설/인프라
inhibit	억제하다
initial	초기
initially	처음에
initiative	선수를 치다
innovation	혁신
inputs	입력

insecurity	불안정
insight	통찰력
instability	불안정
instance	예
institutional	기관적
institutions	기관
insufficient	불충분
insurance	보험
intangible	무형
integrated	집적
integrated circuit	집적회로
integration	통합
intellectual	지식인
intellectual property	지적 재산권
intellectuals	지식인
intense	치열
intensity	강도
intensive	집약적으로
intentionally	의도적으로
interactions	상호 작용
interchangeable	교환할 수 있는
interdependence	상호의존성
interest	이해
interest group	이익 단체
interest rate	이자율
interests	이해
interference	간섭
interferes	방해하다
intermediate	중간
international	외환
international currency	국제 통화
international institutions	국제 기관
international reserve	외환보유고
international system	국제체계
internationalism	국제주의
interpretation	해석
interpreted	이해
intervention	개입
interventionist	개입 주의자
interwar	양 대전 사이
Interwar Period	대전 사이의 기간에
intra-industry	산업 내
invest	투자하다
investigate	조사
investment	투자
investor	투자자
iron ore	철광석
irrigation	관개
is concerned with	와 관련있다
is determined by	에 의해 결정된다
ISI	수입대체 산업화
isolate	고립된
isolation	고립
issue	문제
ITA	국제무역법원
item	물품/품목
ITIC	정보 기술 산업 협의회
ITO	국제 무역 기구
itself	그 자체

J

jeopardize	위태롭게 하다
job	일자리
join forces	협력
join together	함께 결탁
judge	판단

judicial branch	사법부
justice	정의
justification	정당화

K

kept open	개방 유지시키다
key	주요

L

labor	노동
labor market	노동시장
labor scarce	노동력이 희소한
labor union	노동 조합
lack	부족한
lacking	없는
laissez faire	자유방임주의
land-intensive	토지 집약적
landowner	지주
laptop	노트북
last	지속
late developer	후발 개발국
late entrant	후발 진입자
lawyers	변호사
lax	허술한
lay	마련
LDCs	최빈개도국
lead	앞장서가다
lead to	양산
leadership	지도력
legal	법적
legal expense	법적 비용
legislation	법안/입법
legislative body	입법 기관
legitimate	합당한
legitimize	정당화하다
less costly	손해가 덜
less rewarding	보람이 없는
less sophisticated	간단한
lessen	줄이다
level out	변동이 없어지다
levy	부과
liberal	자유주의
liberalism	자유주의
liberalize	자유화하다
liberalizer	자유 주의자
liberty	자유
license	허가
licensed	허용된
life expectancy	기대 수명
lifecycle	수명주기
like-minded	뜻을 함께 하는
limit	제한
limited	제한된
limited role	제한된 역할
linear	선형
linkage	연계
liquid	유동성 있는
liquidate	청산하다
listener	청취자
loan	대출
lobby	로비
lobbyist	로비스트
local	지역

local capital	지방 자본
local industry	지역 산업
locate	둘 수 있게 하다
location	위치/곳에
logic	논리
logical	논리적
logically	논리적으로
logrolling	투표 거래
long term	장기간
lose	잃다
low interest	저금리
low skilled	미숙련
lower cost	값이 더싼 생산자
loyalty	충성

M

machinery	기계
mad cow	광우병
magazine	잡지
magnification	확대
main	주요
mainstay	핵심
maintain	유지하다
major	주요
majority	대다수
make a deal	거래하다
make sure	확인
malnutrition	영양 실조
manage	관리하다
management	관리
manipulate	조작하다
manufacture	제조
manufactured goods	제조품
manufacturer	제조자
market	시장
Marxist	마르크스 주의자
mass produce	대량 생산
mass-consumption	대중소비
masses	대중
mathematics	수학
matter	문제
mature	성숙
maximize	극대화하다
means	수단/방법
measure	지표/측정
membership	회원국
Mercantilism	중상주의
method	방법
MFN	최혜국
middle class	중산층
middle school	중학교
military	군사의
minimal	최소한의
minimize	최소화
Ministerial	각료회의
minority	소수
mislead	속이다
MNC	다국적기업
mobility	유동성
mode	모드
model	모델
moderate	적정
modern	현대
modernization	근대화
modified	조작
momentum	탄력

monetary 통화
monetary system 통화 제도
monitor 감시
monopolize 독점하다
monopoly 독점
morality 도덕
more advanced 선진국
most favored 최혜국 대우
motivated 동기
move 이동
moves 행동
multi-fiber 섬유
multilateral 다자간
multilateralism 다국간주의
Multiple choice 선다형
multipolar 다극
mutual 상호

N

NAFTA 북미 자유 무역 협정
NAM 전미제조업자협회
narrow 좁은
national security 국가 안보
National Treatment 국산품과 같은 처리
nationalist 민족주의
nationalize 국유화하다
natural order 자연 질서
natural product 자연 산물
natural resources 천연 자원
naval 해군
necessary 필요한
necessary condition 필요한 조건
necessary evil 필요악
Negative freedom 부정적인 자유
neglect 소홀히
negotiate 협상하다
negotiated downward 하향 협상
negotiating 협상
neighbor 이웃나라
neither 둘 다 아니다
Neocolonialism 신식민지주의
network 네트워크
neutral 중립적인
NICS 신흥 공업국가
NIEO 신 국제적인 경제 질서
non state 비국가
nondiscrimination 무차별
non-durable 비내구성
non-exclusive 배타적이지 않다
non-producing 비 생산
non-tariff barriers 비관세 장벽
normative 규범적
not much 많지 않다
not necessarily 반드시 그런 것은 아닙니다
notify 알려 드리다
notion 개념
NPR 공영 라디오 방송국
nuanced 미묘한
nuclear 핵
nurtured 육성

O

objective 객관적/목적
obligations 책임이/의무

obstacles 장애물
obtain 얻다
obvious 명백한
occur 생기다
OECD 경제 협력 개발 기구
OEEC 유럽 경제 협력기구
offensive 공격적
offer 제공
offered 제공
offset 상쇄하다
oil 석유
on the other hand 반면에
on their own 독자적으로
one another 서로
one lane 1 차선
one side 한쪽
OPEC 석유수출국기구
open to them 무엇인가를
open up 개방
openness 개방된
operate 운영
opinion 의견
opportunity 기회
opportunity cost 기회 비용
oppose 반대하다
opposite 반대로
oppress 억압하다
optimum 최적
optimum tariff 최적 관세
ordain 정하다
order 질서/순서
organization 조직
organize 조직화
oriented 지향적
originate 유래되다
orthodox 전통적인
otherwise 달리
otherwise do 통상적으로 하지 않는 일을
outcome 결과
outnumber 수가 더 많다
output 생산량/산출량
outsource 위탁하다
over 간
overall 전반에
overcome 극복하다
overestimate 과대 평가하다
overrepresent 대표를 지나치게 많이
oversee 감독하다
overstretch 확장
overturn 반대하다
overvalue 과대평가되다
owner 소유자

P

packaging 포장
panel 패널
panel display 판표시장치
panels 패널
parliament 의회
part 부품
participate 참여한다
particular 특정
pass 통과하다
pass on 부과하다/돌아가다
path 경로
pattern 패턴

payoffs 결과물
peace 평화
peak 최고에
peasant 소농
Peloponnesian War 펠로 폰 네소스 전쟁
per capita income 1 인당 소득
per unit 단위당
perfectly 완벽하게
perform 하다
period 기간
periphery 주변
permanent 영구적인/상설
permit 허용하다/가능케 하다
permitted 허용되는
persistent 지속성 있는
perspectives 관점
persuasive 설득력 있는
petrochemicals 석유 화학
pharmaceutical 제약
phase out 단계적으로 없에온 것입니다
phenomenon 현상
Philosophical roots 철학적 뿌리
philosophy 철학
phrase 구문
piece of pie 파이 조각
place 둡니다
play a part 역할을하다
plenty 많은
point out 지적
policy 정책
political 정치적인
Political Union 정치 연합
politically influential 정치적으로 영향력있는
poll 여론 조사
pollution 오염
poor 가난한
poorest 가장 가난한
poorly endowed 희소한 요소를 가진
population 인구
positive 긍정적인
positive 실증적
positive sum 양의 합계
postwar 전후
potential 잠재적인
poverty 빈곤
power 권력
power plant 발전소
powerful 강력한
practices 관행
practicing law 개업
preclude 배제하다
predict 예측하다
prediction 예측
predominance 우세
preeminent 탁월한
prefer 선호하다
preference 편애
preferences 선호
preferential 특혜의
preoccupy 생각나다
prescriptions 처방전
preserve 보존하다
President 대통령
pressure 압력
presumably 아마
prevalent 보편화된/흔합
prevent 방지
price 가격

price difference	가격 차이
primarily	주로
primary	1차
primary products	1차 생산품
principle	원칙
prison	감옥
prisoner	죄수
private	민간
private gain	자신의 이익을
private sector	민간 부문
privatize	민영화하다
privileges	이득
problematic	문제가 있는
procedure	절차
proceed	진행되다
process	과정
procure	구하다
producer	생산자
product	제품
production	생산
productivity	생산력
products	제품
profit	이익
profit margin	높은 이익
profitable	유익한
progressive	진보적인
proletariat	최하층계급
proliferate	증가
prominent	두드러진/저명한
promote	촉진하다
property right	재산권
proposal	제안
prospect	전망
prosperity	번영
protect	보호하다
protectionism	보호주의
protectionist	보호 주의자
prototype	모형
provide	제공하다
provision	항목
provisionary	임시로
provoke	유발하다
proximity	근접해 있는
public debt	국가채무
public good	공공재
punish	처벌
purchases	구매
purposes	목적
pursue	추구하다
push	밀다
push into	밀어 넣다
push onto	강요하다

Q

qualifications	자격
quantitative	양적인
quickly	빠르게
quota	할당량

R

railways	철도
ramifications	영향
range	범위

range of outcomes 결과의 범위
rapid 빠른
rare 드문
rate 율
rather 보다
ratify 비준하다
ratio 비율
rational 합리적인
raw materials 원료
reach 이르다
react 대응
Realist 현실 주의자
realize 깨닫다
reap 이익을 본다
reason 이유
recent times 최근
recession 침체
reciprocal 상호간의
recognize 인식하다
recommend 제안/권고
record 기록
recover 회복되다
red tape 빨간 테이프
redirected 보내다
redistribute 재분배
reduce 줄이다
refer 참조하다
reflect 반영
reform 개혁
refrigerator 냉장고
refuse 거절하다
region 지역
regionalism 지역주의
regulations 규정
reject 거부하다
relations 관계
relative 상대적인
release 양도하다
relevant 관련된
reliance 의존
religious 종교적인
relocate 이전하다
rely 의존하다
remain 남아있다
removal 제거
renegotiate 재협상
renew 갱신
rent 지대
reopen 재개하다
reorganize 재구성
repay 상환/갚다
repeal 폐지하다
repeat 한번도 없었던 많은
repeatedly 반복해서
replicate 복제하다
report 보고하다
represent 대표하다
representative 대표
reproduce 재현
Republican 공화당
reputation 명성
request 요청
research 연구
research and development 연구 개발
reservation 의구심
reserves 보유고
resolve 해결하다
resource 자원

resource intensive	자원 집약적
respect	존경
respond	대응
responsibilities	책임
rest of	나머지 부분에
restaurants	식당
restraint	규제
restrict	제한하다
restriction	제한
restrictive	제한적인
result	결과
retaliate	보복하다
retaliation	보복
retrain	재교육을 하다
retraining	재교육
retreat	물러서다
return	회귀
return to capital	자본에 대한 수익이
revenue	수익
revert	복귀
reviewed	살펴보다
revision	수정되다
revival	부흥
revolution	혁명
Revolutionary	독립 전쟁
reward	보상
right-wing	우파
rise	출현/인상
risen	상승
risk	위험
rival	경쟁자
rivalry	경쟁
robbery	강도
robots	로봇
role	역할
roots	뿌리
roughly	대략
round	라운드
routine	일상적인 일
RTA	호혜통상협정법/지역 무역 협정
RTAs	지역 무역 협정
rule	규칙
rule of law	법의 지배
rules	규칙
run	운영

S

sacrifice	포기
safeguards	안전 장치
safety valve	안전 밸브
SAL	구조 조정 차관
sales outlet	판매 매장
sanction	제재
sanitary	위생
satisfy	만족시키다
savings	저축
scale	규모
scale of production	생산 규모
scarce	희소한
scarcer	고갈되다
scholar	학자
school of thought	학파
scientific	과학적인
SE	동남
seats	좌석
second best choice	차선책

Secretary of State	국무 장관	significant	크게
section	부분	significantly	상당히
secularize	세속화하다	similar	유사
secure	보호/보안	simplify	단순화하다
Security Dilemma	안보의 고민	simultaneous	동시에
seek	추구한다	single	단일
seize	탈취	single member district	소선거구
select	선택된	site	장
selective	선별적	situation	상황
self-help system	자조 체계	skilled labor	숙련 된 노동
self-interest	이기적인	slice	조각
self-sufficient	자급 자족	sliced up	나뉘어져
semiconductor	반도체	slight	미미
semi-periphery	반 주변	slightly	조금 더
Senate	상원	smarter	똑똑한
serve	공급	social	사회적인
serve their interest	그들의 이익을 증진하다	social unity	사회적 통합
service	서비스	social welfare	사회 복지
set	그것에 해당하는	socialism	사회주의
setting	상황	societal	사회적인
settlement	처리	SOE	국영 기업
several	여러	software maker	소프트웨어 제작자
severe	가혹하게	sophisticate	정교한
shape	모양	sound	확고
share	몫/공동 부담	source	근원
shelter	피난처	sovereignty	주권
shift	이동	speaking	회화
shifting cost	비용을 전가 시키다	special	특별한
ship	배	specialization	전문화
shipbuilding	조선	specific	특정한
shirts	셔츠	spillover	전파
short term	단기	spinning machine	방적기
shortfall	부족	spur	촉진시키다
show	보여 주다	square km	평방 킬로미터

stability	안정
stable	안정적인
staff	직원
stage	단계
stagnate	침체되다
stance	입장
standards	기준
start-up	착수
state	국가
State Department	외무부
state-centric	국가 중심
statistics	통계
status	실태
stay straight	똑바로 가고
steel	강철
steel mill	강철소
steel producer	철강 생산자
steering wheel	핸들
stifle	억압
stimulate	자극하다
stimulate	촉진
stock	재고량
stockpile	비축
stocks	식량축적
straightforward	간단
strategy	전략
stress	강조하다
strict	엄격한
strongly	강력히
Structuralism	구조주의
structure	구조
struggle	투쟁
stuck	갇혀있어
study	연구
sub-assembly	하위 부품을 조립
Subject	주제
submit	제출하다
suboptimal	최적 이하의
subordinate	종속된
subsidies	보조금
subsidy	보조금
substantially	상당히
substitute	대체
successive	연이
suffer	고생
suited	적합합니다
superiority	우위
superpower	초강대국
supplement	보완
supplies	물자
supply	공급
support	지지하다
supposed to	려고
surpass	능가하다
surplus	잉여
survey	설문 조사
survival	살아남다
suspect	의심하다
sustained	오랜
swerve away	침로를 벗어나는
swift	신속한
switch	바꾸다
systematically	체계적으로

T

take into account	고려

take place	일어나다	tie	무승부
talks	협상	tier	계층
target	겨냥/목표	ties	관계
tariff	관세	timetables	시간표
task	작업	timing	타이밍
taste	취향	Tit for Tat	받는 만큼 되돌려 주기
tax	세금	to another	와 다른 한 가지
tax cuts	감세	tolerant	관대하게
tax incentive	감세	tool	도구
tax rate	세율	topic	주제
taxation	과세	toys	장난감
taxes	세금	TPRB	무역정책검토기구
technocratic	기술적 인	Trade policy tools	무역 정책 도구
technology	기술	traditional	전통적인
telecommunications	통신	train	양성
temporary	일시적인	training	훈련
tempting	유혹	transaction	거래
tend	경향이 있다	transaction cost	거래 비용
tenets	신념	transfer	양도
term	용어/기간	transform	변화시키다
terms of trade	무역의 조건	transition	전환
territory	영토	transparency	투명성
testable	시험할 수 있는	transportation	수송
testing	실험	trapped	갇혀 있다
textile	섬유/직물	Treasury	재무부
themselves	자체	treatment	대우
theorem	이론	trend	동향
theorist	이론가	trespassing	무단 침입
therefore	따라서	triumph	승리
these days	요즈음	trusted	신뢰받는
third world	제 3 세계	turn	변환
threaten	압력을 가하다/위협하다	typically	대체적으로
threats	위협		
throughout	내내		

U

ultimately	궁극적으로
unable	할 수 없는
uncompetitive	경쟁력 없는
unconcerned	무관심
unconditionally	무조건
underdevelopment	저개발
undertake	착수하다
unemployment	실업
unequal	불평등한
unequally	불평등하게
uneven	고르지 않은
unfair	불공정한
unfounded	근거 없는
unilaterally	일방적으로
uninterrupted	지속된
unique	독특한
unit costs	단가
unit of analysis	분석 단위
unitary	단일
unity	단일성
unnecessary	불필요한
unprecedented	전례 없는
unregulated	규제되지 않은
unskilled labor	미숙련 노동
unstable	불안정한
unwilling	의지가 없다
up or down	승인 이나 거부
upgrade	개선 시키다
uphold	지키다
urban	도시
urbanization	도시화
use	사용하다
useful	도움이 된
USTR	미국 무역 대표
usually	보통

V

vacant	빈
vague	애매
value	가치
value added	부가가치
values	가치
variable	변수
variants	변종
variety	다양성
vast	광대한
VER	자율 수출규제
versions	버전
victim	피해자
victorious	승전국
view	견해
violate	위반하다
violation	위반
virtue	미덕
visible	선명
volume	양
voluntary	자발적인
vote trading	투표 거래
voters	유권자
VRA	자율 규제 계약
vs	대
vulnerability	취약성

W

wages	임금
waive	보류
wary	경계하는
waste	낭비
watch	시계
waves of	물결
weaken	약화시키다
wealth	부/부유한
wealthy nations	선진국들
weight	가치
welfare	복지
well organized	잘 조직된
what ought to be	무엇이 있어야되는지에
whatever	자기가 원하는 것을
wheat	밀
White House	백악관
widely	넓게
widening	확대
widespread	광범위한
willing	기꺼이
winner	우승자
working class	노동자 계급
working properly	제대로 작동
works best	가장 잘 되다
World Systems	세계 체제
World War II	제 2 차 세계 대전
worry about	걱정하다
worse off	더 불행하다
worthless	쓸모가 없다
would look like	어떠할지
wrong	틀린
WTO	세계 무역기구

Y

yield	양보/다수확

Z

Zero sum	제로섬

James C. Schopf

James C. Schopf is Professor of Political Science at Keimyung University in Daegu, Korea. He received a PhD in Political Science from the University of California, San Diego and a BA from Oberlin College. His research primarily concerns the effects of democratization on corruption, and he specializes in Korean politics. He was among the first to use the newly passed Korean Freedom of Information Act to gather previously classified material for his doctoral dissertation. His articles have appeared in numerous journals including *Asian Survey*, the *Journal of East Asian Studies*, the *Asian Journal of Social Science*, *Pacific Review*, *Korea Observer*, *Telecommunications Policy* and the *Journal of Comparative Asian Development*.